The Economic and Opportunity Gap

The Economic and Opportunity Gap

How Poverty Impacts the Lives of Students

Anni K. Reinking and Theresa M. Bouley

ROWMAN & LITTLEFIELD
Lanham • Boulder • New York • London

Published by Rowman & Littlefield
An imprint of The Rowman & Littlefield Publishing Group, Inc.
4501 Forbes Boulevard, Suite 200, Lanham, Maryland 20706
www.rowman.com

6 Tinworth Street, London SE11 5AL, United Kingdom

British Library Cataloguing in Publication Information Available

Library of Congress Cataloging-in-Publication Data

Names: Reinking, Anni K., author. | Bouley, Theresa M., author.
Title: The economic and opportunity gap : how poverty impacts the lives of
    students / Anni K. Reinking and Theresa M. Bouley.
Description: Lanham : Rowman & Littlefield, [2021] | Includes
    bibliographical references. | Summary: "This book helps teachers and
    other professionals working with students to reflect, improve, and
    implement inclusive practices" — Provided by publisher.
Identifiers: LCCN 2020054130 (print) | LCCN 2021931708 (paper) |
    LCCN 2020054131 (ebook) | ISBN 9781475855845 (cloth) |
    ISBN 9781475855852 (paper) | ISBN 9781475855869 (epub)
Subjects: LCSH: Children with social disabilities—Education—United States. |
    Poor children—Education—United States. | Educational Equalization—
    United States. | Education—Economic aspects—United States. |
    Poverty—United States.
Classification: LCC LC4091 .R4174 2021 (print) | LCC LC4091 (ebook) |
    DDC 371.826/940973—dc23
LC record available at https://lccn.loc.gov/2020054130
LC ebook record available at https://lccn.loc.gov/2020054131

⊗™ The paper used in this publication meets the minimum requirements of American
National Standard for Information Sciences—Permanence of Paper for Printed Library
Materials, ANSI/NISO Z39.48-1992.

Contents

Foreword   vii

Preface   ix

1   What Is Poverty?   1

2   Mindsets   15

3   Theories of Poverty   29

4   Poverty as Trauma   45

5   Homelessness   57

6   Economic Shaming, Food Shaming, Behavior Shaming   69

7   The Importance of Building Positive Relationships and School Climates   79

8   Supporting Ourselves, and Each Other   93

9   Supporting Families: Community Resources and More   103

10   Student-centered Intentional Teaching: Signs of Caring   113

11   Literature-based Lesson Plans: Supporting Students in Poverty   119

References   141

About the Authors   149

Foreword

As a teacher-educator for more than forty years I am very sensitive to the amount of training required of preservice and in-service teachers. From my perspective, texts and other resources must have a blend of solid research combined with an abundance of practical applications throughout. I look for experienced educators who can cite actual field work they have conducted themselves. And the text must be written in accessible language. Anni K. Reinking and Theresa M. Bouley exceed in all these areas.

I had two major first impressions upon reading this book. First, the staggering statistics and research data that will certainly raise the eyebrows of the most jaded educator. Reinking and Bouley report the typical comments of educators or community members when asked to define or associate words to "poverty." Many of the responses are uncomfortably revealing—dirty, hungry, charity, depression, fear, violence, and starvation. The text serves to challenge educators to uncover their beliefs and values about the poor and "how poverty impacts our students, the classroom, the community, and relationships."

The second impression I had was the theme of humanity that comes across the entire work. "About 15 million children in the United States—21% of all children—live in families with incomes below the federal poverty threshold, a measurement that has been shown to underestimate the needs of families." And, "Poverty does not see religion, race, ethnicity, gender, sexuality, location, or behavior." The Unites States has one of the highest rates of poverty compared to other rich countries. Reinking and Bouley help expand our understanding of what poverty means and how we as educators must exam our perspectives. "Educators' views of students and/or families are often one of two ways: a deficit-based mindset or an asset-based mindset."

We are cautioned about "overwhelmingly focusing on the students' problems rather than the strengths of the student."

Chapter 3, "Theories of Poverty," was particularly fascinating reading. Reinking and Bouley provide one of the most succinct explanations of the Ruby Payne versus Paul Gorski theories of poverty. They relay Payne's "culture of poverty" as a way to improve support based on individual realities. Yet, her lack of empirical data and overgeneralizations based on stereotypes result in subjective interpretations which detract from the quality and personalization of her work: by focusing on the flaws of the "culture of poverty" and disregarding the lack of equal opportunities.

Other chapters provide very helpful insights and suggestions on dealing with the trauma of poverty, understanding, and helping homeless students, and building a strong community school. Chapter 7, "The Importance of Building Positive Relationships and School Climates," describes an effective strategy to ensure that each child receives the support and attention they need. The text later provides guidance in dealing with compassion fatigue or teacher burnout. Other chapters provide a comprehensive understanding of the issues accompanied by a helpful listing of resources and strategies. Reinking and Bouley have clearly researched and analyzed the issues of poverty and the effects on students. Most importantly they provide us with a much deeper understanding of the connection between poverty and schooling and what we as educators must know to better serve an often-marginalized population.

New as well as veteran educators will find *The Economic and Opportunity Gap: How Poverty Impacts the Lives of Students* a valuable addition to their teaching toolbox.

William A. Howe, EdD
Past president, National Association for Multicultural Education (NAME)

Preface

While the official journey to writing this book began in 2016, the ideas and research have always been bubbling in the minds of both authors. However, when Dr. Reinking began teaching at a state university in Illinois, she was tasked with developing a course for practicing teachers focused on working with students in poverty due to the high rate of poverty in school districts around the university. Dr. Reinking successfully developed a course, with the help of great colleagues, and provided a completely online course focused on working with students and families living in poverty.

For three years she facilitated/instructed the course; however, she knew she wanted to share the knowledge her students were getting to a wider audience. So, of course, a book!

Dr. Reinking and Dr. Bouley connected through their common research in multicultural education and at annual meetings of the National Association for Multicultural Education (NAME), and began writing this informative, important, and timely book for educators at all grade and experience levels. In NAME's 2016 publication, *Multicultural Education: A Renewed Paradigm of Transformation and Call to Action*, NAME identified LGBTQ+ populations and rural poverty as the two areas of multicultural education that are most lacking of research. This book answers their call to action and will contribute greatly to the absence of research on rural poverty.

While this book has a great deal of information, ideas, and resources, what stands out the most and is a foundational starting place is the reality that nearly one-fourth of our children in the United States are living in poverty, a whopping 21 percent. This number, one that is doubled in some communities and does not consider children in families near the poverty line, is striking when compared to other similarly situated countries. Further, this excerpt from chapter 1: *A common misconception is that poverty impacts families of color more and/or urban populations. However, poverty does not discriminate. The highest increase in poverty rates has occurred in rural counties in the United States. Many of the rural counties with the biggest increase in poverty levels are 97 percent white, while others are predominately Black American, demonstrating that rural poverty crosses demographics.*

As you read this book, we ask that you reflect, discuss, and learn. This is a guide, a resource, and something to add to your already-overflowing teacher toolbox. Yet, and perhaps most importantly, we hope that you explore ways to work together to eradicate poverty in your community because lowering the national poverty level starts at home.

Chapter 1

What Is Poverty?

The word "poverty" comes from the French word "poverte," which means poor. But, poverty is much more than "just being poor." "Poverty is a multifaceted concept of social, economic, and political elements" (Kumar, 2018).

When you do an internet search for "What is poverty?" several results are populated:

Poverty is . . . the state of being extremely poor.
Poverty is . . . the state of being inferior in quality or insufficient in amount.
Poverty is . . . not having enough money for basic needs (food, drinking water, shelter).
Poverty is . . . hunger.
Poverty is . . . lack of shelter.
Poverty is . . . being sick and not being able to see a doctor.
Poverty is . . . not having access to school and not knowing how to read.
Poverty is . . . not having a job, fearing for the future, and living one day at a time.
Poverty is . . . losing a child to illness brought about by unclean water.
Poverty is . . . powerlessness, lack of representation, and freedom.

When you ask a room of educators or community members to define or associate words to "poverty," you may hear such words as dirty, poor, homeless, hungry, unemployed, charity, depression, fear, violence, and starvation.

Regardless of the definition, personal or professional, poverty, as is evident in research and reality, cannot be easily defined. Poverty has many causes and consequences, which will be discussed throughout this book. Additionally, we will discuss poverty through the lens of an educator. We will discuss how poverty impacts our students, the classroom, the community, and relationships. We will also discuss teacher reflective practices, instructional strategies, and provide lesson plans based in literacy as a way to provide windows and mirrors into the classroom based in economics.

WHO IS LIVING IN POVERTY?

While the statistics vary depending on the definition and focus of the research, the National Center for Children in Poverty (NCCP) states,

> About 15 million children in the United States—21% of all children—live in families with incomes below the federal poverty threshold, a measurement that has been shown to underestimate the needs of families. Research shows that, on average, families need an income of about twice that level to cover basic expenses. Using this standard, 43% of children live in low-income families.
>
> (www.NCCP.org) (We will discuss how the poverty line is determined in the next section.)

Below is another example of how poverty has been reported in the United States. Figure 1.1 is a graph displaying the "percentage distribution of public school students, for each racial and ethnic group, by school poverty level: Fall 2017."

As you can see in figure 1.1, poverty does not discriminate. Poverty does not see religion, race, ethnicity, gender, sexuality, location, or behavior. Poverty can happen to anyone, at any time, sometimes with only one or two decisions or events that impact financial stability.

A common misconception is that poverty impacts families of color more and/or urban populations. However, poverty does not discriminate. The highest percent of poverty occurs in rural counties around the United States. While poverty levels in urban areas have slightly decreased, poverty levels in rural areas have experienced a steady incline for years. Additionally, the U.S. Census bureau found that poverty levels increased 30 percent in many rural

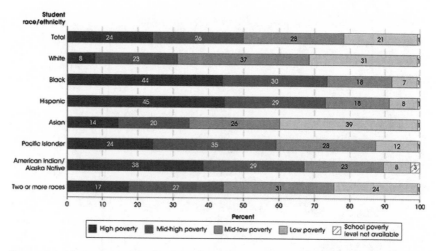

Figure 1.1 Percentage Distribution of Public School Students for Each Racial and Ethnic Group by School Poverty Level, 2017. *Source*: https://nces.ed.gov/fastfacts/displ ay.asp?id=898.

counties in each state from 2016 to 2018. During the same time the overall poverty rate dropped 1 percent, varying from state to state. Many of the rural counties with the biggest increase in poverty levels are 97 percent white (i.e., Carter County, Kentucky, had one of the biggest increase up 8.5 points to 31.31) while others are predominately Black-American (i.e., Alabama poverty levels grew in 27 of 67 counties with some counties increasing by as much as 10 points), demonstrating that rural poverty crosses demographics (Henderson, 2019).

Poverty also does not discriminate by age. American elderly are at risk with more than 10 percent of Americans over sixty-five living in poverty. When considering supplemental poverty the number substantially increases. Furthermore, the percentage of grandparents and great grandparents raising grandchildren has increased, which can contribute to the percentage of students living in poverty. It has been stated that 2.6 million grandparents are raising their grandchildren due to various circumstances. This leads to a disproportionately high rate of poverty among grandparents, with more than 40 percent having reported economic or social service needs that are unmet (Henig, 2018).

Further statistics compare the United States to other rich countries. In this comparison, the United States has one of the highest rates of poverty compared to other rich countries (see figure 1.2).

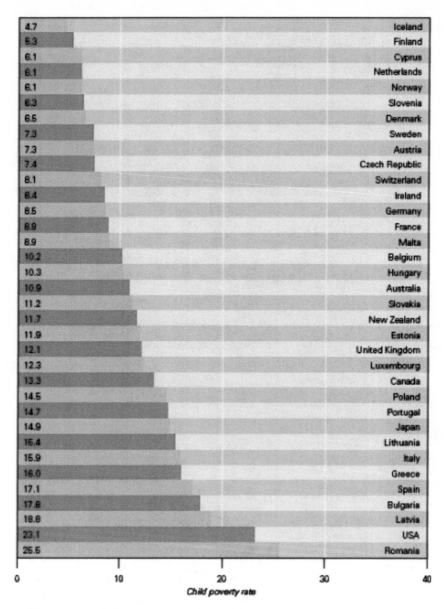

Figure 1.2   **UNICEF Child Poverty Rate by Country.** *Source*: https://www.commondreams.org/news/2012/05/30/unicef-us-among-highest-child-poverty-rates-developed-countries.

Regardless of the statistics or the reasons, when discussing children, the experience of poverty can impact a child for a lifetime.

After all that being said, what is the definition of poverty used in this book? It is a combination of several definitions. In order to provide readers with a common understanding, here is the definition of poverty the authors will be using as we move through this book:

> Poverty, through the lens of an educator, is an experience for students that involves free and reduction lunch, and/or an inability to pay activity/field trip fees, and/or instability in housing, and/or instability in food security, or/and eligibility for Title I, and/or hygiene difficulties (due to a lack of running water, laundry services, etc.).

While this is not an exhaustive list, it does prime you, the reader, to think about what poverty may look like in schools and in the lives of students.

THE POVERTY LINE

Poverty, in the eyes of the United States, is defined through numbers. Specifically the numbers related to the income level for families based on a formula designed in 1963–1964 by Mollie Orshansky, based on survey data from 1955 (the latest available at that time). The formula was developed to essentially "allow" each family to spend one-third of their household income on food. Originally Orshansky developed the poverty thresholds based on the economy food plan or the cheaper of the four food plans developed by the Department of Agriculture. Additionally, this plan and threshold were originally designed "for temporary or emergency use when funds were low" (Fisher, 1997) because she determined, on average, how much is too little to survive.

While very minor changes have been made since the original development of the threshold, the changes that have been made are still based in 1963 costs and living conditions. The Census Bureau uses the Official Poverty Measure (OPM) which compares pretax cash income against the minimum food diet in 1963. However, noticing the obvious disregard for changing economics, the Census Bureau introduced the Supplemental Poverty Measure (SPM) in 2010. While the SPM did not replace the OPM, it does provide a wider

Table 3. Poverty measure concepts differ between the official poverty measure and the Supplemental Poverty Measure.

Poverty Measure Component	Official Poverty Measure	Supplemental Poverty Measure
Measurement Units	Families (see note) or unrelated individuals	Resource units (official family definition plus any coresident unrelated children, foster children, and unmarried partners and their relatives) or unrelated individuals (who are not otherwise included in the family definition)
Poverty Threshold	Three times the cost of a minimum food diet in 1963	Based on expenditures of food, clothing, shelter, and utilities (FCSU)
Threshold Adjustments	Vary by family size, composition, and age of householder	Vary by family size and composition, as well as geographic adjustments for differences in housing costs by tenure
Updating Thresholds	Consumer Price Index: All items	Five-year moving average of expenditures on FCSU
Resource Measure	Gross before-tax cash income	Sum of cash income, plus noncash benefits that resource units can use to meet their FCSU needs, minus taxes (or plus tax credits), minus work expenses, medical expenses, and child support paid to another household

Figure 1.3   Side-by-Side Comparison: OPM and SPM. *Source*: L. Fox, "The Supplemental Poverty Measure: 2016," Current Population Reports P60-261 (RV), Revised September 2017.

picture of poverty in the United States using different measurement units. Figure 1.3 is a side-by-side comparison of the OPM and the SPM.

If school personnel are interested in poverty threshold simulations, there are three resources listed below:

1. Spent http://playspent.org/.
   In this simulation, participants attempt to make it through a month through the eyes of someone living at or below the poverty line.
2. What is Poverty? https://www.tolerance.org/classroom-resources/tolerance-lessons/what-is-poverty.
   In this Teaching Tolerance lesson, participants "explore the causes of poverty in the United States and the factors that perpetuate it." The four lessons aim to challenge the idea that poverty is simply the result of individual shortcomings. Students will examine the ways poverty is closely related to economic and political policy, and will work to discover why it disproportionately affects members of nondominant groups—that is, groups that have historically been oppressed.
3. Figuring poverty level: https://www.apa.org/pi/families/poverty.

Reflection: After completing or reading some of the above resources, what was surprising? What is something you will use in your classroom?

TYPES OF POVERTY

There are various ways to identify or describe types of poverty based around the idea of poverty being a social, economic, and political aspect of our world. However, before discussing the types of poverty, ensuring all readers have a basic understanding of Maslow's Hierarchy of needs is imperative.

Maslow's Hierarchy of Needs focuses on what individuals need psychologically in order to fulfill innate human needs (Huitt, 2007). Maslow based the hierarchy on two groupings: deficiency needs (first four levels) and growth needs (last four levels).

According to Maslow, if an individual does not have their deficiency needs met, then the individual cannot move onto the growth needs. The first four levels (deficiency) are physiological, safety/security, belongingness and love, and esteem. Essentially, if an individual is deficient in one of the basic needs the individual will strive to remove that deficiency. The growth needs include cognitive, aesthetic, self-actualization, and self-transcendence. Figure 1.4 is a visual description of Maslow's Hierarchy of Needs.

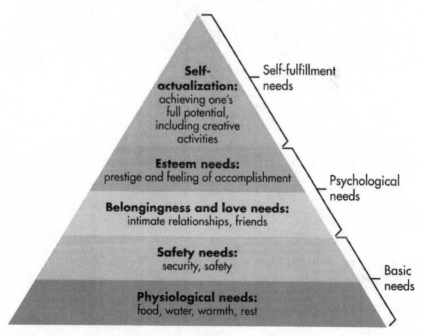

Figure 1.4 Maslow's Hierarchy of Needs. *Source*: https://www.simplypsychology.org/maslow.html.

To understand how the levels interact and impact our lives, here is an excerpt from an informational description of Maslow:

> Individuals at the lowest level seek coping information in order to meet their basic needs. Information that is not directly connected to helping a person meet his or her needs in a very short time span is simply left unattended. Individuals at the safety level need helping information. They seek to be assisted in seeing how they can be safe and secure. Enlightening information is sought by individuals seeking to meet their belongingness needs. Quite often this can be found in books or other materials on relationship development. Empowering information is sought by people at the esteem level. They are looking for information on how their egos can be developed. Finally, people in the growth levels of cognitive, aesthetic, and self-actualization seek edifying information (or information that improves an individual in some way: morally, educationally, or spiritually). (Huitt, 2007, para 6)

Maslow's Hierarchy of Needs is important to understand because most poverty types lack in one or more of the areas humans need to feel secure.

We will dive into each of the nine types of poverty listed below; however, it is important to remember that while this list is long, it is not exhaustive. The types of poverty are also not listed in any specific order.

However, before discussing the types, we will discuss the concept of economically disadvantaged and low socioeconomic status (SES).

Economically Disadvantaged: A student or family who is economically disadvantaged is socially kept out of systems due to economic hardships. Specifically, an economically disadvantaged student is a student whose household income is below average. They, along with other types of students living in poverty, may not be able to pay the extra money for a field trip or for a book order. Generally speaking, an economically disadvantaged student in the eyes of school districts is a student who qualified for free or reduced lunch under the National School Lunch and Child Nutrition Program (will be discussed in a later chapter).

Some researchers refer to economically disadvantaged individuals as socially and economically disadvantaged, which displays the interconnectedness of economic gain with social prosperity. For example, a student who is never able to get an extra book at the book fair or pay the extra money for a field trip is socially ostracized by schools around the country.

All of the types of poverty intertwine with economically disadvantaged.

Low SES is an individual or group of people who are lower, in this case financially has less, than other groups that are being compared (i.e., people in society). Often low SES is discussed in terms of students in schools.

A low SES student is a student with "lower educational achievement, poverty, and poor health" (APA, 2019). Additionally there has been research over the years stating that children who live in low SES environments lack language and reading development, have fewer books at home or overall literacy in their environments, and have less stimulating toys to play with (Aikens & Barbarin, 2008; Bergen, Zuijen, Bishop, & Jong, 2016; Bradley, Corwyn, McAdoo, & García Coll, 2001; Orr, 2003; Buckingham, Wheldall, & Beaman-Wheldall, 2013) (table 1.1).

Absolute/Extreme Poverty

Robert McNamara, the former president of the World Bank, defines "absolute poverty as a condition so limited by malnutrition, illiteracy, disease, squalid surroundings, high infant mortality, and low life expectancy as to be beneath any reasonable definition of human decency" (2019).

Absolute or extreme poverty is generally associated with individuals living in third world countries where there are numerous preventable diseases causing deaths (malaria, cholera, etc.). Referring back to Maslow's Hierarchy of Needs, people living in absolute poverty lack physiological needs, such as food, shelter, and clean water, as well as some safety needs (Kumar, 2018). Due to this lack of physiological and safety needs, individuals living in absolute poverty are often focused on surviving day-to-day.

While absolute poverty is uncommon in developed countries, it does not mean that it is not possible or does not exist. Lack of running warm water, heat, or quality health care could arguably be a type of absolute poverty experienced in the United States.

Table 1.1 Types of Poverty

Economically Disadvantaged	
Low Socioeconomic Status	
Urban	Environmental
Generational	Absolute/Extreme
Situational	Relative
Working-Class	Rural
Asset	

Relative Poverty. Relative poverty is not defined from a purely economic point of view, but rather in terms of a social context (Kumar, 2018). For example, if families who are in your neighborhood or group of friends are able to buy presents for their children at holidays, but you are unable to, that is relative poverty—relative to your in-group or reality. Therefore, in this situation, relative (or compared to) to your neighbors you would be considered poor. In a phrase often used, "Are you able to keep up with the Joneses?"

Situational Poverty. A family or individual living in situational poverty is generally the result of an adverse situation or event (Kumar, 2018), such as job loss, divorce, or a house fire. In this type of poverty, the lack of funds is only for a short window of time as the family or individual recovers financially from the adverse event. Sometimes in situational poverty, families will seek assistance from community agencies or churches for a onetime, get back up on your feet, financial support.

Generational Poverty. Generational poverty is "passed on" from generation to generation. While this might lend readers to think of poverty as a "cycle," that is not the case with generational poverty. Generational poverty stems more from the access to, knowledge of, and availability of resources and tools to plan for the future rather than living day by day or month by month.

While a child cannot choose which zip code they are born into, often the zip code determines the level of poverty a child experiences. It is known as being "born into poverty." Generational poverty is defined as a family where "at least two generations have been born into poverty" (Jensen, 2009). When that occurs, it has been found that the family is "not equipped with the tools to move out of their situation" (Jensen, 2009). With that being said, it does not mean that once in generational poverty families have no hope of escaping, it just means more assistance and resources will be needed to facilitate the families process to a less impoverished experience.

Rural Poverty. When a rural area is defined as an area that has characteristics of a countryside as compared to a town setting. A rural setting has a population of less than 50,000. In rural areas there are "less job opportunities, less access to services, less support for disabilities, and quality education" (Kumar, 2018). In such rural areas, Maslow's Hierarchy of Needs are often not met due to the lack of transportation to community organizations or social service agencies where there are resources. Therefore, needs are not met due to lack of transportation and the distance that is often quite far (too far) to walk. Overall, rural poverty is when needs are not met due to lack of jobs, lack of financial security or support, and a lack of access to resources.

Urban Poverty. An urban area, which is defined as an area that is developed in or around a city and has a population of more than 50,000, where major financial and social challenges are present. Due to the high cost of living in most urban areas, urban poverty relates to individuals who have limited access to health care and education, mostly due to environmental and political factors, inadequate housing and services, violent and unhealthy living conditions, and minimal social protection (i.e., policy presences) (Kumar, 2018). The urban poor deal with a complex aggregate of chronic and acute stressors, including overcrowding, violence, and noise, which are often not addressed by inadequate city service departments (Jensen, 2009).

Environmental Poverty. Many times factors of environmental poverty overlap with factors in urban poverty due to the lack of healthy air quality and noise in urban areas. The term "environmental poverty" was coined by Liu in 2012 when discussing environmental factors contributing to poverty in China. However, environmental poverty or the impact of the environment on low SES (socioeconomic status defined below) communities in the United States is also prevalent.

For example, in a podcast titled *The City*, the hosts bring to light the story of Chicago's North Lawndale environmental poverty in the spring of 1990. For some background, according to the 1990 census, North Lawndale ranked ninth in percent of people living below the poverty level (eight community areas were poorer and 68 were richer) and also in the percent of children living below the poverty level. One neighbor, Ms. Woodson, began noticing dump trucks coming in and out of the neighborhood during all hours of the night. Eventually the dumping became apparent from the thirteen-football-field-sized lot that was reaching a tipping point.

What was being dumped? Debris from a construction and concrete company operating in high-end parts of the city. By the time the lot was filled to the brim, there was a constant cloud of dust over the neighborhood, rats carrying diseases climbing in and out of the debris, and the spot became an eyesore for the community. Children were diagnosed with asthma, older adults were having trouble breathing, and people were experiencing constant headaches and nosebleeds. Although there were complaints and an eventual FBI case, it took several years, decades, to clean up the environmental mess created in this impoverished neighborhood. A neighborhood whose residents relied heavily on public assistance for health and transportation needs. That is just one example of environmental poverty. The long-standing water issue in Flint, Michigan, is another, and one that may be most publicized.

This one example can be seen replicated around the country and is often described in two ways: (1) grow first, clean up later, or (2) out of sight, out of mind. The second saying refers to the idea that marginalized or impoverished communities are often "not seen" by the wider community, therefore their issues are not seen and therefore not important to policymaker or other individuals in the wider society.

Working-class Poverty. This is also known as the "working poor." People who are classified into this category are people who spend twenty-seven weeks or more a year in the labor force either working or looking for work, but whose incomes fall below the poverty level (Center for Poverty Research, University of California, Davis). Essentially, the working poor are people who are working and contributing to society however do not make enough to live above the poverty line.

In 2017 Sen. Bernie Sanders's Government Accountability Office conducted a research study and found that 20 percent of working families earning the $7.25 minimum wage or below (in 2017) live in poverty. Senator Sanders coined this group of individuals as living in a situation of "starvation wage(s)" when this report was released. Working-class poverty can occur in any type of community and impact any demographic of family.

A story that is often told in the news or on social media that describes a type of family that is working-class poor revolves around the narrative of workers at corporate locations that are not paid a living wage, not given health care, and cannot afford childcare. Often a corporate giant that is pulled into the discussion is Walmart. In a 2018 article discussing Walmart and the employees of Walmart falling below the poverty line, the following statements were made (McCarthy, 2018):

> The corporate giant is raising the hourly minimum wage across its stores to $11 from $10, as well as giving out one-time bonuses that will net its longest-serving employees up to $1,000. The company will also expand its paid maternity leave program to 10 weeks.
>
> The improvements will still not lift full-time Walmart workers above the federal poverty line.
>
> Although the increase at Walmart will be welcomed by employees across its 4,700 stores, $11 an hour translates to roughly $22,000 a year for a full-time worker, below the federal poverty line of $24,600.

This provides a picture of individuals working full-time, but still not making enough to survive based on a poverty line that was set in the 1960s.

Asset Poverty. A situation where families/individuals have minimal to no assets to rely on in the event of a financial disruption or shock, such as job loss, medical crisis, or needed home or vehicle repair. It has been found that more than 63 percent of American children and 55 percent of Americans live in asset poverty (Klampe, 2019). When families have financial assets, such as a home, investments, or vehicles, being able to use (i.e., sell) those assets to help make it through a financial crisis provides a safety net or "insurance" against unexpected life events.

Assistant Professor David Rothwell stated, "This is a dimension of financial security that we don't think about that much, and it's pretty high. The findings highlight the extent of financial insecurity among American families. These shocks ripple through the family and down to the children." Through his research Professor Rothwell found, "A growing body of research suggests that parents' asset levels also predict academic achievement, educational expectations and likelihood of college enrollment and graduation. Families with assets that can be used when income is disrupted are also likely to experience less financial stress and strain" (Klampe, 2019).

CONCLUSION

Poverty comes in many forms and has many adverse effects on students and families as they grow and move through life. However, it is also important to remember that bringing in the ideas of asset-based thinking and funds of knowledge is critical to our work with students and families living in poverty. This may be difficult to know if we aren't aware of our own biases and beliefs, and how they compare to the facts. In the next chapter we discuss these mindsets and misconceptions.

Reflect on the following statement: Economists estimate that child poverty costs an estimated $500 billion a year to the U.S. economy; reduces productivity and economic output by 1.3 percent of GDP; raises crime and increases health expenditure.

(Holzer et al., 2008)

Chapter 2

Mindsets

Ask us why the poor are poor, and we have a response quick at the ready, grasping for this palliative of explanation. Rather than hold itself accountable, America reverses roles by blaming the poor for their own miseries.

—Matthew Desmond

Everyone has images and/or words that come to mind when they engage in conversations, it is human nature. However, when discussing people living in poverty, the mindsets or thought processes from society tend to be negative. Such as, poor people are lazy or poor people do not care about their kids' education because they never come to school for conferences or events. Knowing these negative mindsets often permeate through society and school buildings, this chapter focuses on how to change deficit-based thinking to asset-based thinking. More specifically, how to recognize biases, explicit or implicit, that can impact the way educators and peers interact with students and families living in poverty.

To begin our journey of changing a deficit-based mindset to an asset-based mindset regarding students and families living in poverty, we are going to address some common myths and misconceptions about people living in poverty (table 2.1).

Reflection: What are some other ideas around poverty you've heard? Are they true? How do you know?

15

Table 2.1 Misconceptions and Reality of People Living in Poverty

Myth/ Misconception	Reality/Fact
Poverty doesn't exist in America	"About 15 million children in the United States—21% of all children—live in families with incomes below the federal poverty threshold, a measurement that has been shown to underestimate the needs of families" (NCCP, 2019). *Reflection: Do a quick search and compare the number of children living in poverty in the United States as compared to other developed countries.*
Poor people are lazy and unmotivated	Over half of the people in the United States who are living in poverty are either too old or disabled to work or too young to work. Additionally, some people living in poverty work, usually full-time, but are still considered the "working poor." Therefore, there are underlying conditions preventing individuals from working that have nothing to do with their work ethic, drive to succeed, or strength. Over and over that poverty stems not from a lack of initiative, but from a wide scope of other factors including low wages, lack of jobs, poor school quality [low expectations and inequitable opportunities], high childcare costs, a racialized criminal justice system and discrimination in the labor market (Brandpoint, 2018). *Reflection: What is your familiarity with this misconception? How would you refute this argument in a conversation? Where does this mindset come from?*
Few U.S. children are homeless	More than 1.6 million of the nation's children go to sleep without a home each year. Homeless children experience a lack of safety, comfort, privacy, reassuring routines, adequate health care, uninterrupted schooling, sustaining relationships, and a sense of community. These factors combine to create a life-altering experience that inflicts profound and lasting scars (National Center on Family Homelessness, 2012). *Reflection: Do a quick search and compare the number of children who are homeless in the United States as compared to other developed countries. What is our collective obligation in eliminating homelessness?*

(Continued)

Table 2.1 Misconceptions and Reality of People Living in Poverty (*Continued*)

Myth/ Misconception	Reality/Fact
All children have equitable opportunities to succeed	Not all children have the resources or opportunity to succeed later in life due to economic opportunities. Statistics show that 32 percent of children who live over half of their childhood in poverty do not graduate from high school. Many other factors need to be considered when stating that all children can succeed. Remember, children living in poverty may be malnourished, experience higher levels of stress or trauma, which impacts their brain development, or the fact that many low-income, high poverty schools have a high turnover rate of teachers or teachers with less experience (Social Work Degree Center, 2019). *Reflection: How can we make our educational system more equitable?*
Poverty does not have a long-lasting impact on children	As will be evident throughout this book, this is overwhelmingly false. Poverty has an intense and long-lasting impact on children throughout their entire lifetime. The poverty experienced today is not a countrywide poverty, it is a poverty stemming from inequity. Children who live in poverty are at an extremely high risk for mental and physical disorders, due to lack of nutrition, physical stimulation, and/or emotional development (Social Work Degree Center, 2019). *Reflection: Reflecting on the students in your classrooms who live in poverty, what are some of the impacts you have observed?* *How can educators inform the general public and politicians about the negative impact poverty has on students' academic and social development?*

MINDSETS

All mindsets often stem from experiences, background, and knowledge gained through interactions in various parts of one's life.

Asset-based and Deficit-based

Educators' views of students and/or families are often one of two ways: a deficit-based mindset or an asset-based mindset. Some argue these two

Table 2.2   Asset-Based Approach to Students

Asset-Based Mindset	Asset-Based Classroom Example
Strengths driven	(Student comes into school ten minutes late.) I am so glad you came to school today. We love when you are here and learning as part of our community.
Opportunity focused	You have the opportunity to learn today with your peers.
Internally focused	You did the right thing, even when no one was looking!
Funds of knowledge (What is present that we can build upon?)	You have very focused and determined opinions and insights on this topic. Let us use that passion and knowledge when we write our information text.
Could lead to new and unexpected response	Wow, your questions and insight really sparked a great conversation in class today. I think everyone learned something from you today, even me! (Building confidence.)

concepts are dichotomous while others argue this relationship is not solely dichotomous but more of a spectrum. Regardless, these two ways of thinking about students and families (deficit- and asset-based), specifically in relation to students and families who are living in poverty, can be points of strength or points of destruction in a classroom environment. Tables 2.2 and 2.3 provide an explanation, with examples, of the asset-based approach and the deficit-based approach (University of Memphis, 2019).

As you can tell from these tables, it is a mindset change and a verbal engagement change.

A deficit-based mindset or way of thinking is focusing on the things that are wrong. For example, "That student never has their homework done" or "That student is always smelly and not clean." This mindset is many times where the misconceptions discussed earlier flood our thinking and therefore impact our actions and words.

Arguably, elementary classrooms that implement the clip system (i.e., color system) feed into the deficit-based mindset by overwhelmingly focusing on the students' problems rather than the strengths of the student. When a student is constantly being left out of "good kid" celebrations or their name is never on the wall for excelling, the downward cycle of depression and lack of motivation begins. This can also occur in middle school and high school grades when students are never recognized for the work they are doing independent of what others are doing—not comparing but rather seeing personal growth.

Table 2.3 **Deficit-Based Approach to Students**

Deficit-Based Mindset	Deficit-Based Classroom Example
Needs driven	(Student comes into school ten minutes late.) You are late and you obviously did not care how you looked or smelled today. You need to clean yourself.
Problem focused	You can't seem to ever focus in the classroom, so you have to work by yourself.
Externally focused	You were not following directions, go move your clip on the clip chart.
	You did not do what I asked, you have to sit out of recess now.
What do we (educators) need to fix?	You seem to not be able to be quiet in class, we have to fix that.
	You can't sit still, I need to fix that because it is distracting.
Could lead to depression or low self-esteem	We do not have time to hear your story/opinion (never follow back up with student). (Student decreases in confidence.)

Conversely, asset-based thinking focuses on the good, or what is right. For example, "That student asked to complete their homework before school in my room" or "That student showed up to school today." Some scholars synonymously refer to asset-based thinking as funds of knowledge. Specifically, funds of knowledge are the skills and knowledge (the what) that students bring with them into a classroom that reflect their historical and cultural knowledge of functioning in society (Moll, Amanti, Neff, & Gonzalez, 1992).

Walking hand in hand with asset-based thinking and funds of knowledge is the concept of a growth mindset. A growth mindset is encapsulated in the understanding that the brain is malleable and with guidance and opportunity, "anything is possible." It is the idea that a skill comes from opportunity and practice. Essentially, educators with growth mindsets embrace the idea that their students can succeed, therefore providing equitable opportunities. An educator without this mindset limits students' access to specific resources or academic rigor because students are not "smart enough" and will never make it out of the poverty they were born into.

Implicit and Explicit Bias

While it would be fantastic if we all could be reflective on our personal asset and deficit-based mindsets, it is not that easy. Sometimes our mindsets or biases are apparent (explicit) and sometimes our mindsets or biases are hidden to our own reflection (implicit).

But what is a bias? A bias is both a verb and a noun. As a verb, bias means that something causes you to feel or show inclination for or against one person or a group of people. In the example based around the concept of this book, it may be that you show favoritism to students who are clean and well-fed when they come to school. As a noun, bias means prejudice in favor of or against a person or group of people. In the example based around the concept of this book, it may be that you hate people who live in poverty because they are all lazy and smelly (refer back to table 2.1 at the beginning of this chapter).

It is important to understand, however, that some of our biases are conscious (explicit) and some of our biases are unconscious (implicit). Either way, it is our duty as educators to ensure that our biases do not negatively impact any student in our classroom or school environment.

Explicit biases are those attitudes and beliefs we have about specific people or a group of people that is at our conscious level. While personally we are aware of these explicit biases, it often is embarrassing to share due to political correctness or a fear of displaying an -ism (i.e., racism, ageism, etc.).

Implicit biases are those attitudes and beliefs that we have about specific people or a group of people that is at our unconscious level. Most of our biases are at this level, especially without deep reflection or introspection. Since implicit biases are unconscious we cannot disclose them because we are unaware of them. However, if you are interested in discovering your own implicit biases, the Implicit Association Test is a well-regarded test to help individuals make conscious the unconscious.

Reflection: We all have implicit biases and being aware of what they are is an important first step to not acting on them. What are your implicit biases? Do you know where they originated?

Associated to the idea of bias, specifically implicit bias is the theory/concept known as the Ladder of Inference. This idea was coined by Chris Argyris (1982) and used by Peter Senge (2014) in *The Fifth Discipline: The Art of Practice of Learning Organization*. This ladder or theory displays the fact that our beliefs have a big impact on how we select from reality, which can also lead us to ignore the true facts. Essentially, this way of thinking, which all humans do instinctively, can create a vicious circle. The ladder can be used in several ways, but these are the two ways we will discuss:

1. Challenge personal beliefs/actions.
2. Challenge other's beliefs/actions.

In figures 2.1 and 2.2 the Ladder of Inference and an example from an educators' mind/view are displayed.

Observable data: A student does not bring their permission slip or homework back to school (figure 2.2).

Reflection: Think about a negative or deficit-based mindset you may have or you have seen colleagues display. Go through the Ladder of Inference, starting at the bottom rung. Once done, reflect on how that process changed or did not change your thinking.

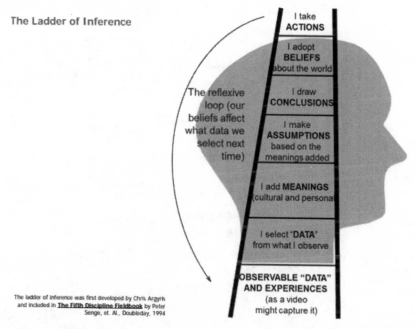

Figure 2.1 The Ladder of Inference. *Source:* Model Developed by Chris Argyris (blog, trainerswarehouse.com).

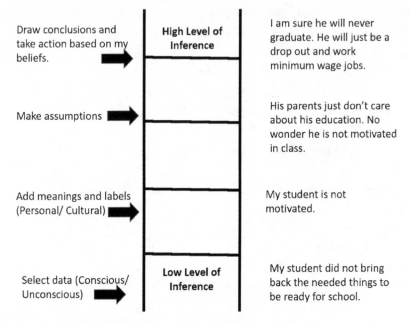

Draw conclusions and take action based on my beliefs.	**High Level of Inference**	I am sure he will never graduate. He will just be a drop out and work minimum wage jobs.
Make assumptions		His parents just don't care about his education. No wonder he is not motivated in class.
Add meanings and labels (Personal/ Cultural)		My student is not motivated.
Select data (Conscious/ Unconscious)	**Low Level of Inference**	My student did not bring back the needed things to be ready for school.

Figure 2.2   Example of The Ladder of Inference. *Source*: Created by A. Reinking, 2019.

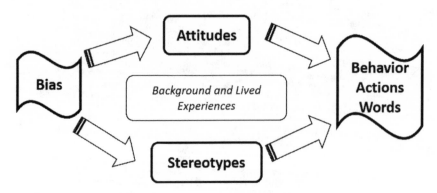

Figure 2.3   Bias Leading to Behavior, Actions, and Words. *Source*: Created by A. Reinking, 2019.

Regardless if our biases are conscious or unconscious, they impact our classrooms and school environments. Therefore, personally reflecting on actions and words is imperative (figure 2.3).

ANTIBIAS ACTION STEPS

If we have recognized personal biases or mindsets, what can we do? Well, while there are several steps educators can take, beginning with the process of reflection and developing an action plan, the other steps include work that is often exclusively discussed in the field of early childhood education: Antibias Curriculum.

> Anti-bias teachers are committed to the principle that every child deserves to develop to his or her fullest potential. Anti-bias work provides teachers a way to examine and transform their understanding of children's lives and also do self-reflective work to more deeply understand their own lives. (Derman-Sparks & Edwards, 2010, page 2)

Derman-Sparks (1989) coined the term and designed the foundational aspects of Antibias Curriculum. She based the foundation of her work on the idea that "young children are aware that color, language, gender, and physical ability are connected to privilege and power. Racism and sexism have a profound influence on children's developing sense of self and others" (1989, p. 161). Therefore, Antibias Curriculum focuses on the assets of each student while also helping students to understand differences and develop a sense of self in relation to the world around them. The overall goal of Antibias Curriculum is to build students, families, and educators who can confront and eliminate barriers of prejudice, misinformation, and bias about specific aspects of personal and social identity (Teaching for Change, 2019).

Within Antibias Curriculum, there are four goals:

1. Each student will demonstrate self-awareness, confidence, family pride, and positive social identities.
2. Each student will express comfort and joy with human diversity; accurate language for human differences; and deep, caring human connections.
3. Each student will increasingly recognize unfairness, have language to describe unfairness, and understand that unfairness hurts.
4. Each student will demonstrate empowerment and the skills to act, with others or alone, against prejudice and/or discriminatory actions.

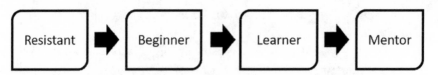

Figure 2.4 Trajectory of Antibias Reflection and Implementation *Source*: Revised by A. Reinking, 2019, based on Derman-Sparks, LeeKeenan, & Nimmo, 2015.

Overall, the activities, goals, and foundations of the Antibias curriculum "pay attention to the realities of children's [student's] lives" (Derman-Sparks & Edwards, 2010).

As we consider the work of early childhood teachers through the lens of Antibias Curriculum, I hope you, the readers, can see how these concepts can cross over into elementary, middle, and high school grades. All children, regardless of age, need this type of education with educators who are also willing to learn.

However, there is a trajectory for teachers who are ready for this work across to teachers who are not quite ready for this work in their classroom or school building. While they are not mutually exclusive, teachers often move through the process in a linear pattern. However, teachers can also be at different places in their process for different topics/areas (figure 2.4).

A "resistant" teacher "seems uncomfortable talking about diversity and talks or acts in discriminatory ways" (Derman-Sparks, et.al., date, p. 44). They also have expressed objections to diversity and/or the inclusion of multicultural education or culturally responsive teaching in the classroom/ school building. An example of a teacher in the resistant stage might complain of students/families speaking in their home language at the school (non-English). Another example of a resistant teacher may be vocal complaints of students who do not pay for field trips due to socioeconomic constraints.

A "beginner" teacher "seems unaware of or has little experience with different social identities" (p.44). A teacher at the beginner stage may make comments focused on difference-denial. For example, "We are all the same, I do not see X (color, socioeconomic status, gender, etc)."

A "learner" teacher "is open to talking and thinking about diversity and is willing to take on new challenges" (p. 44). A teacher who is at the learner stage is open to discussions, seeks out answers, and is willing to learn and implement new ideas into the classroom for the benefit of students and families. While the "learner" teacher is open to learning, an educator at this stage does not take an activist stance but rather observes and takes in information. For example, a "learner" teacher may seek answers on how to best educate students living in poverty, but does not change the cost of classroom activities, does not change the expectations of financial participation, or does not have discussions/lessons with students regarding socioeconomics.

Finally, a "mentor" teacher "has expertise and experience" (p. 44) in diversity/multicultural education, both professionally and/or personally. Teachers in this stage are important allies, activists, and help school buildings move forward with change. Educators in this stage offer suggestions, assist colleagues in their learning stage, and ensure that the school implements culturally responsive teaching strategies in the classroom and throughout the entire school building. For example, mentor teachers may actively find grants or other monetary donations to assist in financial burdens many families experience when trying to pay for school supplies and activities.

Reflection: As a self-reflective educator, which stage are you currently in regarding students living in poverty or students who have socioeconomic struggles? Think about colleagues and answer the same question.

CULTURALLY RELEVANT AND RESPONSIVE TEACHING

Within the field of multicultural education there are two ideas, which are often used in tandem or synonymously (referenced earlier), that do not directly link to the concepts of poverty but are important to the overall classroom environment for all students, including those living in poverty. The two concepts are culturally relevant pedagogy and culturally responsive teaching, which is a part of the multicultural education umbrella. How are these two concepts different? One encompasses the other.

Pedagogy encompasses teachers because pedagogy is the act of teaching. The pedagogy adopted by teachers shapes their actions, judgments, and other teaching strategies by taking into consideration theories of learning, understanding of students and their needs, and the backgrounds and interests of individual students. Therefore, since the two terms are intertwined, they will be defined in conjunction with each other.

While we will argue against the idea of poverty as a culture, it is important to recognize the disproportionality of ethnic minorities living in poverty.

"Among racial and ethnic groups, African Americans had the highest poverty rate, 27.4 percent, followed by Hispanics at 26.6 percent and whites at 9.9 percent. 45.8 percent of young black children (under age 6) live in poverty, compared to 14.5 percent of white children" (Economic Policy Institute, 2019). Now that we have the same base knowledge, it is important to focus on the tenets of culturally responsive teaching as a way to reach all students, including students living in poverty because the goal of CRT is to create a learning environment conducive to all people entering a classroom/school environment, no matter their ethnic, cultural, or linguistic backgrounds (Frey, 2010).

Gloria Ladson-Billings (1995, 2001) coined the term "culturally relevant pedagogy," which is the act of implementing culturally relevant pedagogy. In her definition or outline, she dictated that it includes teachers who:

1. hold high academic expectations
2. demonstrate cultural competence, the understanding that their own worldview and understandings may or may not align with those of their students
3. are sociopolitically aware, that is, they have a willingness to acknowledge and critique inequity.

Additionally, culturally relevant pedagogy includes inviting voices into the classroom that are generally overlooked or marginalized in texts and curricula throughout schools in the United States (Fink, 2016). Marginalized populations include many groups of people, but specifically for this book, we will focus on the silenced population of students and families living in poverty. Geneva Gay, a well-renowned researcher in the field of culturally responsive teaching, discusses the inclusion of marginalized voices into the classroom. Gay (2013) states,

> Culturally responsive teaching requires replacing pathological and deficient perceptions of students and communities of color with more positive ones. While the problems and challenges these populations face in society and schools must be addressed they should not be the only emphases. (p. 54)

Incorporating culturally relevant/responsive teaching into a classroom or school environment means recognizing and celebrating those students who show up to our classrooms daily, welcoming their voices, demanding their reflection, and encouraging them toward self-discovery. It means creating an environment that has both "windows and mirrors." A mirror is a story that reflects your own culture and helps you build your identity. A window is a resource that offers you a view into someone else's experience.

Overall, it is critical to understand that students cannot truly learn about themselves unless they learn about others as well. It also means that you as an educator are responsive, which means to react quickly and positively with openness and receptiveness. Openness to hear about students' lives, incorporate students' realities into the classroom, and solidify classroom and school interactions in an assets-based mindset.

Information for reflection: "Countries are often judged by the way they treat their children. Poverty in early years can have long-lasting consequences on various dimensions of children's future lives, including their adult health status, their performance at school, and future labor market outcomes" (Smeeding & Thevenot, 2016). According to the OECD (Organisation for Economic-Cooperation and Development), the United States has the highest child poverty rates found among the youngest children.

For instance, the child poverty rate of children younger than six years in the United States was 24 percent in 2010 compared with 21 percent for all children younger than eighteen years. The comparable overall poverty rate for all persons is 17 percent.

Reflection: What does this mean for our classroom communities? What is in the locus of control for the educator/school when we have statistics that represent high child poverty rates?

Chapter 3

Theories of Poverty

We hear a lot of talk about achievement gaps these days, and rightfully so. America has only grown more diverse, but the gaps have barely closed at all. When we discuss achievement gaps, we need to understand that they're more than just percentages on a screen. The gaps we see in achievement for different groups of students are just symptoms of an underlying problem: opportunity gaps.

—Keven Welner

Theories are often used as a way to understand a phenomenon or concept. Theories are fact-based frameworks that present an idea. However, for most phenomena there are many theories depending on evidence, ideas, and research. The concept of poverty is no different. There are several theories that focus primarily on the concept of poverty, several theories that touch on the concept of poverty, and even more theories that do not directly link to poverty but can be used as a framework for educators working with children and families living in poverty. In this chapter theories from each of these three categories will be described and discussed.

RUBY PAYNE VERSUS PAUL GORSKI

If you have searched, googled, or attended professional development that focuses on working with students living in poverty, the topic probably focused on the theory developed by Ruby Payne. However, as will be evident in this section, there are some concepts Ruby Payne promotes that are degrading to families and students living in poverty. An up and coming researcher, who is critical of Ruby Payne's ideas, is Paul Gorski. Both of these leading researchers will be discussed, and both focus on students living in poverty and the intertwined nature of poverty and education.

In this section, we are going to include voices from students who were part of a summer graduate course for educators that focuses on working with students and families living in poverty. It is a five-week online course. The students cover many concepts, which was the genesis of this book. One main concept the students learn about in the course revolves around Ruby Payne and Paul Gorski, especially since many of the students have participated in training based in Ruby Payne's framework. After researching and reading books and articles focused on the two researchers, the students are instructed to write a paper that analyses the relationships between (compare and contrast) the two researchers. Therefore, as a way to describe Ruby Payne and Paul Gorski, we will be providing excerpts from the students' work.

Ruby Payne

Ruby Payne is best known for her books *A Framework for Understanding Poverty* and *Bridges Out of Poverty*, as well as her work on the concept of poverty as a culture and the impact of that culture of poverty in education. One of her foci is the idea of the "hidden rules" of social classes, outlined in the next section.

Hidden Rules among Social Classes, Ruby Payne

After the graduate students read excerpts, listened to podcasts, and did independent research, they wrote analysis papers. Below includes some of those excerpts (table 3.1).

Student 1 [Culture of Poverty]: Payne portrays many of the stereotypes with people who live in poverty. She puts adults and children into a "poverty bubble" and makes them [all] out to have the same culture, obstacles, and mindsets.

Student 2 [Language of Poverty]: Payne uses the shortcomings of people in poverty as the reason that they struggle to move out of poverty. For example, she states that people in poverty use casual register when speaking

Table 3.1 Hidden Rules among Social Classes, Ruby Payne

	Poverty Class	Middle Class	Wealthy Class
Possessions	People.	Thing.	One-of-a-kind objects, legacies, pedigrees.
Money	To be used and spent.	To be managed.	To be conserved and invested.
Personality	Entertainment; sense of human is highly valued.	Acquisition and stability; achievement is highly valued.	Connections—financial, political, and social are highly valued.
Social Emphasis	Social inclusion of people liked.	Emphasis is on self-governance and self-sufficiency.	Emphasis is on social exclusion.
Food	Quantity important: Did you have enough?	Quality important: Did you like it?	Presentation important: Was it presented well?
Clothing	Valued for individual style and expression of personality.	Values for its quality and acceptance into norm of middle class. Label important.	Clothing valued for its artistic sense and expression. Design important.
Time	Present most important. Decisions made for moment based on feelings or survival.	Future most important. Decisions made against future ramifications.	Traditions and history most important. Decisions made partially on basis of tradition and decorum.
Education	Valued and revered as abstract but not as reality.	Crucial for climbing success ladder and making money.	Necessary tradition for making and maintaining connection.
Purpose	Believes in fate. Cannot do much to mitigate chance.	Believes in choice. Can change future with good choices now.	Generosity and nobility toward those less privileged.
Language	Casual register. Language is about survival.	Formal register. Language is about negotiation.	Formal register. Language is about networking.
Family structure	Tends to be matriarchal.	Tends to be patriarchal.	Depends on who has money.

(Continued)

Table 3.1   Hidden Rules among Social Classes, Ruby Payne (*Continued*)

	Poverty Class	Middle Class	Wealthy Class
Worldview	Sees world in terms of local setting.	Sees world in terms of national setting.	Sees world in terms of international setting.
Love	Love and acceptance conditional based upon whether individual is liked.	Love and acceptance conditional and based largely upon achievement.	Love and acceptance conditional and related to social standing and connections.
Motivation	Survival, relationships, entertainment.	Work, achievement.	Financial, political, social connections.
Humor	About people and sex.	About situations.	About social faux pas.

in formal settings like school or work because they have not been taught how to speak in formal register. Because of that shortcoming, people in poverty struggle to get or keep jobs.

Student 3 [Overview]: Ruby Payne pulls at heartstrings by generalizing characteristics that make society want to save those in poverty. Her analysis of language registers, resources, and hidden rules are meant to provide insight for social agencies and schools into the "culture of poverty" as a way to improve support based on individual realities. Yet, her lack of empirical data and overgeneralizations based on stereotypes, result in subjective interpretations which detracts from the quality and personalization of her work. By focusing on the flaws of the "culture of poverty," and disregarding the lack of equal opportunities, resources, and environmental conditions conducive to economic advancement, Payne's framework is incomplete.

Student 4 [Overview]: Payne uses stereotypes to define her classes, she lumps people into poverty based on how she thinks the group at large reacts to things like, money, food, time, education, and family structure (2009, p. 44). She makes the assumption that those in poverty view money as something that should be used, not managed as in the middle class or invested as in the wealthy. She draws on scenarios which portray those in poverty as women-headed households and their children and children's children living in the moment and relying more on relationships within their defined class than outside agencies providing assistance (Payne, DeVol, & Smith, 2009).

Reflection: What do you notice about the students' reactions to Payne's work?

Paul Gorski

In a 2018 presentation by Paul Gorski, one statement stuck out more than any other. He was first introduced to the work of Ruby Payne by a colleague who gave him one of her books. When reflecting on this situation he stated, "I thought it [the book and concept of the culture of poverty] was satirical." Essentially, he thought the information provided by Ruby Payne in her book was a spoof and not something that she (or others) actually thought.

Paul Gorski is best known for his work focused on multicultural education. In relation to this book, his work focused on students living in poverty is summarized in the book *Reaching and Teaching Students in Poverty*, which is part of a larger collection supported by well-known researcher James Banks. The foundational tenet of Gorski, as compared to Payne, is the fact that Gorski adamantly states there is no culture of poverty. There is not a culture of poverty that focuses on weak work ethics, unmotivated individuals, high rates of abuse and addiction, and linguistic deficiencies, all of which are proselytized through Payne's work.

Just as before, after the graduate students read excerpts, listened to podcasts, and did independent research, they wrote analysis papers. Below are some excerpts from those papers.

Student 1: Gorski begins Reaching and Teaching Students in Poverty with an Introduction in which he acknowledges the plight of the teacher and administrator when it comes to providing education to families in poverty. He states, what I have been thinking when reading all of these articles, "it is not my job to ensure that every student has healthcare and high-quality preschool" (2013, p.2) and he does not scold this way of thinking. He acknowledges that teachers are being held accountable for the result of the effects of poverty on the students seen through high-stakes testing.

Student 2: Gorski (2001) states that relational strategies might be even more important than practical strategies because they guide the day-to-day decisions we make as educators. They [relational strategies] also can be harder than more practical strategies to implement because they require us to honestly examine our biases and predispositions about poverty and people living in poverty. Gorski's book, "Reaching and Teaching Students in Poverty" made me look at my own biases I may have of some of my parents. I realize that this may be affecting my relationships with a few students. I really need to focus on seeing the "whole" student. Gorski believes that when we take time to get to know students hopes, fears, and interests; we are able to learn about their families on an individual basis.

Student 3: Gorski takes the stand that poverty exists everywhere and with any type of person, whether they are from the inner city or suburbs, and no matter if they are White, African American, or Hispanic. I appreciate the hopefulness of Gorski's message. Change can happen, even if it is in small doses and in simple ways. One of the first ways is to eliminate those stereotypes that Payne seems to focus on.

Student 4 [Opportunity Gap]: Gorski looks at the inequality of society and the schooling system as the reason people in poverty are at a distinct disadvantage [also known as the opportunity gap]. An example of this would be schools in the city of Chicago having less resources and opportunities compared to the wealthy suburban Chicago schools.

Student 5 [Opportunity Gap]: The split of classes according to Gorski is done so in regard to their access to financial resources, not their culture (2013, p.7). Instead of trying to dissect the mannerisms of these groups and how one should go about communicating with them in response to these mannerisms, Gorski identifies what the lower economic classes need to succeed. He establishes an "Equity Literacy" which hopes to address the biases and inequities in the classroom (Gorski, 2013). When Gorski focuses greatly on the equity of schools. He says that things should not be equal, but instead equitable. Gorski defines equal as fair, so in essence spreading an equal amount of resources among school districts, when in reality that poverty stricken school districts need things to be equitable, or the same for each district (2013, p.20).

Student 6: Paul Gorski looks at transforming institutions based on empirical data instead of long held myths that increase the class divide. He also champions characteristics of resiliency among people living in poverty, and focuses on inequities within society which impede progress. His focus is not on fixing those in poverty, but rather on helping social reformers and policy makers in recognizing, responding to, and redressing inequities that hold individuals back from breaking the cycle of generational poverty. Gorski's approach does not point to the individuals as flawed, but to the inequities within society and our education system that limit the resources available for upward economic mobility.

Reflection: What do you notice about the students' reactions to Gorski's work? In comparing the two sets of reactions, what do you find similiar and/or different? In comparing the two, what comes to mind?

Payne versus Gorski

While Payne and Gorski are not in complete opposition to every concept focused on students (and families) living in poverty, there are many foundational pieces of each researcher that are in conflict. Table 3.2 provides those differences.

The graduate students also provided summaries or direct comparisons of Payne and Gorski. Here are some of their final reflections.

Student 1: Payne uses sweeping generalizations to describe people in poverty. For example, Payne discusses the hidden rules of poverty and then generalizes that to all poor people. However, Gorski divides the poverty group up and distinguishes within the group women, children, racial diversity, etc. Gorski points out that not all people in poverty are created equal.

Table 3.2   Payne vs. Gorski

Payne Foundational Positive Practice	Gorski Direct Criticisms
Holding all students to high expectations.	Focus on individual interventions and ignore the systems that cause, worsen, and perpetuate poverty.
Finding and focusing on students' cultural assets rather than their perceived deficits.	Overgeneralize about people living in poverty and rely upon stereotypes.
Providing curricular mirrors so students can see themselves in the classroom materials.	Focus on perceived weaknesses (or deficits) of children and families living in poverty.
Getting to know students' families and communities.	Theoretically undergrounded and offer little evidence that they work.
Allowing students to share narratives about their lives	Process workshops and their price tags, capitalize on the needs of children in poverty.

Payne on the other hand discusses the "culture of poverty" in her book and makes claims to know about what characteristics men, women, and children have who live in poverty. Gorski's rebuttal to this "culture of poverty" is that "the culture of poverty idea is nonsensical because the idea that we can know anything about somebody based on a single dimension of her or him is, in the end, nonsensical." Payne sees people in poverty more as a group, whereas Gorski sees them more individually.

Student 2: One similarity I saw between Payne and Gorski is that they both address stereotypes in their book. Each of them talks about myths that exist about people in poverty and then explains the reality of the situation. I do feel as if Gorski does a better job of pointing out stereotypes. I feel as if Payne points some stereotypes out in some parts of her book but then actually stereotypes poor people herself in other parts of the book.

The next similarity I noticed is that they both offer strategies and advice on how to best help and communicate with students and people in poverty. They both discuss the importance for teachers to have high academic expectations for all students, avoid bias learning material, make curriculum relevant to student's lives, and discuss the fact that inequity and biases exist and be willing to have an open and honest conversation about it.

Student 3: Both writers [researchers] show empathy towards people experiencing a life in poverty and I believe that both want to better the educational system to provide more opportunity and access to quality instruction and resources to all children, regardless of class. I've enjoyed reading material and research from both Payne and Gorski (Gorski a little more) because they are both a part of the same cause: helping students in poverty to receive equitable education and better educational opportunity.

Student 4: Payne (2001) states that for adults from poverty, the primary motivation for their success will be their relationships. People from generational poverty who desire to function well in middle class usually create new support systems. However, Gorski takes the relationship theory a step farther as he believes the only way to form a healthy relationship is to look within yourself first. He teaches people to look at their personal biases that have been embedded in them.

Student 5: [Overall], student Payne focuses on a script to be used by social workers or other agencies when speaking with those in poverty, unlike Gorski who speaks to a teacher's role in supporting those in poverty.

ADDITIONAL THEORIES

As Gorski and Payne are often referred to when discussing theories of poverty, specifically related to education, there are other hypotheses, theories, and perspectives that are important to consider when planning, engaging, and reflecting as an educator.

Economic Concepts

Five economic concepts will be discussed, all of which relate to poverty. The first is the Permanent Income Hypothesis (PIH). The second is the Life-Cycle Hypothesis (LCH). The third is the Absolute Income Theory. The fourth is the Relative Income Theory. Finally, the Broken Windows Theory will be described and discussed.

The PIH is an economic theory attempting to describe how agents spread consumption over their lifetimes. First developed by Milton Friedman, it supposes that a person's consumption at a point in time is determined not just by their current income but also by their expected income in future years—their "permanent income." In its simplest form, the hypothesis states that changes in permanent income, rather than changes in temporary income, are what drive the changes in a consumer's consumption patterns. In the PIH model, the key determinant of consumption is an individual's lifetime income, not his current income.

Permanent income is defined as expected long-term average income. A consumer's permanent income is determined by their assets: both physical (shares, bonds, property) and human (education and experience). These influence the consumer's ability to earn income. The consumer can then make an estimation of anticipated lifetime income. A worker saves only if they expect that their long-term average income, that is, their permanent income, will be less than their current income.

Reflection: Reviewing that definition of what PIH is, consider how this might relate to the lifetime and/or income of a family living in poverty. Is this a theory that is applicable to everyone and every family? Why or why not? Stating this theory, and understanding that many people's beliefs in the United States are implicitly based in this concept, how might this influence interactions?

The LCH focuses on the saving and spending habits of people over the course of their lifetime. The theory, developed by Modigliani and Brumberg in the early 1950s, postulates that people plan their spending over the course of their lifetimes, factoring in their future income, which results in a bell curve over one's lifetime. The LCH replaced an earlier theory developed by Keynes in 1937, known as the Keynesian Theory, which postulated that as incomes grow, savings would grow, which was generally refuted by LCH.

Combining the two concepts of PIH and LCH, researchers have found that understanding families living in poverty is difficult. These theories are not adaptable to individuals living in poverty or individuals whose incomes change to the negative in their lifetime. Therefore, while these concepts are still used in the financial world, therefore influencing overarching mindsets in society, they are not appropriate to use as a foundation.

The Absolute Income Theory concerns how a consumer divides his disposable income between consumption and saving. Absolute income does not take into consideration those other factors, but simply reflects the total amount of earnings you've received in a given period.

The Relative Income Theory states that an individual's attitude to consumption and saving is dictated more by his income in relation to others than by abstract standard of living; the percentage of income consumed by an individual depends on his percentile position within the income. Relative income measures your income in relation to other members of society, weighing it against the current standards of the day.

Reflection: As discussed in chapter 1, there are also the concepts of absolute and relative poverty which are adjacent to the concepts of relative and absolute income. As a way to reflect and develop a deeper understanding of these concepts, take time to compare, contrast, and relate these ideas.

There is one more theory that is often associated with economics. It is known as the Broken Windows Theory. It was originally researched in 1969 by a Stanford University psychologist, Philip Zimbardo. After leaving two cars, one in an affluent neighborhood and one in an impoverished neighborhood, it was observed that the car in the impoverished neighborhood was destroyed, beginning ten minutes after parking in the neighborhood, while the car in the affluent neighborhood was untouched. However, Zimbardo decided to take the research one step further: he smashed the window of the car in the affluent neighborhood. Once the window was smashed, the car in the affluent neighborhood ended up much like the car in the impoverished community, it was destroyed (Hidden Brain, 2016).

Based in Zimbardo's research, criminologists Kelling and Wilson proposed the Broken Window Theory (McKee, 2020), by taking the small idea of one car in a neighborhood to an entire neighborhood. Eventually, what they found was similar. In neighborhoods where homes were unkempt or had literal broken windows, crime rates and incarceration rates went up. However, in neighborhoods where homes were cared for, even if they were abandoned, crime rates and incarceration rates were low. Their conclusion? Spend time and money to prevent or take care of small crimes and then major crimes in neighborhoods will be reduced (Hidden Brain, 2016).

This concept relates to families and students living in poverty because, since this concept was introduced, there have been more arrests in impoverished neighborhoods. In a Hidden Brain (podcast) episode, it was stated,

> Police ramped up misdemeanors for things like smoking marijuana in public, spraying graffiti and selling loose cigarettes. And almost instantly, they were able to trumpet their success. Crime was falling. The murder rate plummeted. It seemed like a miracle.

While the initial results were visibly positive, in the last fifteen to twenty years, this concept has been argued and critically dismantled because of the community impact, including but not limited to, the impact of low-income communities.

PERSPECTIVES

Aside from theories, which often unconsciously guide overarching societal views, there are also mindsets that are based in fields outside of education. Perspectives from the field of medicine and social work are just a couple that educators can dive into. In this section we will discuss the strengths-based perspective, related to asset and deficit mindsets (chapter 2), as well as a theory known as the asset theory. Additionally, we will touch on the concept of the resilience theory, as it is related to the strengths-based perspective.

Strengths Perspective

The Strengths Perspective, beginning in the 1980s, is an approach to social work that puts the strengths and resources of people, communities, and their environments, rather than their problems and pathologies, at the center of the helping process. It was created as a corrective and transformative challenge to predominant practices and policies that reduce people and their potential to deficits, pathologies, problems, and dysfunctions.

The Strengths Perspective emphasizes the human capacity for resilience, resistance, courage, thriving, and ingenuity, and it advocates for the rights of individuals and communities to form and achieve their own goals and aspirations. While acknowledging the difficulties that individuals experience, the Strengths Perspective never limits people to their traumas (chapter 4), problems, obstacles, illnesses, or adversities. Instead, social workers (educators) address individual experiences as challenges to grow problem-solving skills, opportunities, and motivators of change. Overall, it is a perspective of empowerment for individuals who are facing challenges, such as living in poverty (KU, School of Social Welfare).

There are three main principles of the Strengths Perspective for educators when working with individuals, students, and families.

1. Recognize that every individual, group, family, and community has strengths (i.e., funds of knowledge) and resources (i.e., capitals).
2. Realize that while trauma, abuse, illness, and struggle may be injurious, they may also be courses of challenge and opportunity (i.e., problem-solving).
3. Engage with individuals, students, and families with a sense of caring and hope.

Reflection: How can educators embrace these principles when working with students living in poverty?

Resiliency Theory

What is resiliency? Easily defined it is the act of "bouncing back." According to the American Psychological Association (APA), resilience is the process of adapting well in the face of adversity, trauma, tragedy, threats, or even significant sources of risk. Therefore, the theory of resiliency is that adaptations individuals make in their lives when facing challenges. Resiliency is often discussed in relation to children and their ability to adapt to adversity through experiences and the impact on brain development (chapter 4).

The following are the core questions at the heart of Resiliency Theory:

1. What is the difference for children whose lives are threatened by disadvantage or adversity?
2. How is it that some children successfully overcome severe life challenges and grow up to lead a competent and well-adjusted life?

Everyone experiences challenges or adverse situations in their lives, but some individuals shut down in the face of adversity while others do not. Why? Brain development, resiliency, and coping strategies.

Individuals who have the internal building blocks to bounce back to a state of normalcy relatively well after a traumatic experience have developed resiliency. Furthermore, some people even use their trauma to propel them into a more satisfying life as compared to before the traumatic experience. While it would be nice if we had one clear answer as to why some people have resilience and some do not, there currently is no clear way to answer this. However, researchers are working on finding the "magic."

One professor at the Institute for Child Development at the University of Minnesota, Ann Masten (2001), coined the term "ordinary magic" to describe the mix of ingredients that make resilience. In her book *Ordinary Magic: Resilience in Development*, Masten discusses the origin of resilience theory, what it means, and the process of gaining resilience. Specifically, Resiliency Theory is rooted in the study of adversity. During World War II scientists were curious about how children were reacting to the stress of war. The war brought poverty, homelessness, disease, starvation, and death. Scientists from all over the world were eager to research the impact of severe trauma on children (Masten, 2001).

For forty years, Masten studied children around the world throughout their life. She discovered common traits (the magic) among resilient children who have faced adversity. She figured out that resilience is a combination of what she calls "ordinary factors" such as their relationships, family, and individual differences such as personality and even genetics (Masten, 2001).

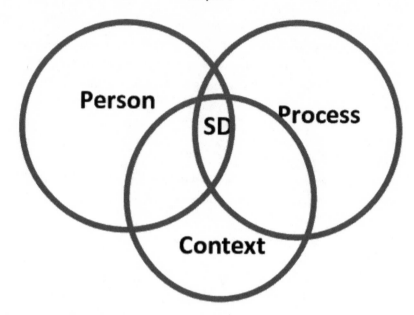

Figure 3.1   Person Process-Context Model. *Source*: Created by A. Reinking, 2019, based on Michael Rutter, 1987.

Another researcher, Michael Rutter (1987), discovered that resilience is better explained in terms of processes and used the Person Process-Context (PPC) Model. This model made it easier for researchers to study the correlation between risk and protective factors. The PPC Model is displayed in figure 3.1 (SD = Self-Directed).

The following are the six significant predictors of resilience, as outlined by Rutter (1987):

1. Stressors—these activate the resilience process and create a disruption in homeostasis in the individual, family, group, or community. The perception of stress can vary because of the person's viewpoint.
2. The external environmental context—this includes the balance of risk and protective factors in the child's environment such as school.
3. Person-environment interactional processes—this is the process between the child and their environment. The child either passively or actively tries to understand and overcome demanding environments to build a more protective situation.
4. Internal self characteristics—this is the spiritual, cognitive, behavioral, physical, and emotional strengths needed to be successful in different tasks, cultures, and environments.

5. Resilience processes—this is the short-term or long-term resilience or coping processes learned by the individual through gradual exposure to increasing challenges and stressors that help the individual to bounce back (Richardson, Neiger, Jensen, & Kumpfer, 1990).
6. Positive outcomes—successful life adaptation regardless of stress, risks, and traumatic experience means that a person has a higher chance of success when faced with negative events later on in life.

Overall, the Resiliency Theory and the Strengths Perspective both focus on the positives, the strengths, the assets of the individual as a way to grow, change, and learn.

CAPITALS

Capitals, in reference to individuals, include all of the aspects of one's life that assists in further social and economic gains. There are several types of capitals that will be discussed. Specifically, social, cultural, and human.

Social capital is the ability to seek the needed resources to build a strong supportive circle, in the school and wider community. These circles or networks (social capital) are developed as a way to be successful in the long term. Social capital, or the ability to acquire access to resources through connections between individuals or membership in social networks and other social structures, is key to confronting obstacles creating a pathway to successful adaptation and acculturation (Portes & Rumbaut, 2001).

Cultural capital relates to an individual or family identity as it relates to the nonfinancial social assets that promote social mobility (Olneck, 2000). Assets that promote social mobility beyond economic means include education, intelligence, speech, and dress. This is often influenced by educators' mindsets, comments, and experiences designed for the classroom environment. Cultural capital, in reference to education, refers to the family values that facilitate access to education (Portes, 2000).

According to Portes and Rumbaut (2001), human capital refers to the skills that students and parents bring in the form of education, work experience, and language knowledge that make individuals productive at home, school, and work, which also could be referred to as their funds of knowledge (Moll, Amanti, Neff, & Gonzalez, 1992).

Table 3.3   What Are Your Capitals?

	Human	
Social		Cultural

Educators, through identification in research, need to focus on the use of the cultural and human capital (modes of incorporation). Modes of incorporation include how the community allows or denies families use of their human and cultural capital to promote successful economic and social adaptation.

The human, cultural, and social capitals of all families and students are at the core of the equity lens. Ensuring that the skills and knowledge all students, including those living in poverty, bring to the classroom are valued and accepted, educators developing a full understanding of the educational experiences, community experiences, and daily family experiences of students is imperative to the student inclusion.

Reflection Activity: Fill table 3.3 to reflect on your own capitals. What are the capitals that are part of your life and community?

What are your "capitals"?

Chapter 4

Poverty as Trauma

Impoverished children are climbing mountains before they can walk.

(FiresteelWa, 2019)

In general, poverty is when needs are not met for all household members. In this chapter we will discuss how poverty impacts children's brain development due to lack of nutrition, safety, attachment, stability, and health care. All of which contribute to the experience of trauma.

Trauma? Isn't trauma something "extreme"? Isn't trauma something that changes the trajectory of someone's life? Isn't trauma distressing? Yes, the answer to all of those questions is yes. Now go back and ask yourself the same questions changing out trauma for poverty. The answers are still yes. Poverty is "extreme" depending on the person. Poverty can change the trajectory of an individual's life. And, poverty is distressing, stressful, and painful.

Therefore, in this chapter we will discuss the impact of poverty on brain development. We will also discuss the concept of poverty as a trauma. Finally, the chapter will end with common reactions or behaviors that students may display in the classroom with the underlying cause related to brain development, trauma, and possible lack of coping strategies.

BRAIN DEVELOPMENT

The brain has been researched for generations; however, in the last decade, more and more research has led to a better understanding of how the brain in children works and how it develops. When a baby is born, their brain contains all of the brain cells, or neurons, they will have for the rest of their life. The environment decides how those brain cells are nurtured and through interactions, connections are made. Specifically, the prefrontal cortex is the part of the brain that educators are "working" on constructing through the whole educational trajectory. What should be noted is that researchers have determined that the prefrontal cortex does not fully develop until the early to mid-twenties.

Brain development in infancy and early childhood lays the foundation for all future development. During this time, from birth until age five, a child's brain develops more than at any other time in their life (First Things First, 2019). In percentage terms, the child's brain grows 90 percent before beginning kindergarten.

Therefore, the quality of a child's experiences in these first years of life, regardless if they are positive or negative, shape the brain for the rest of the individual's life. It has been found that the relationships children have with individuals around them (adults) are essential to developing healthy or unhealthy brain connections. The goal of all relationships is to be consistent and caring so the child is able to form healthy connections in their brain, which will impact the present and future life. "Most children living in chronic toxic stress (i.e. poverty) will experience a detrimental change in how their brain works" (firesteelwa.org).

Figure 4.1 is a graphic demonstration that displays the impact of poverty on the brain, as designed by Early Hearing Detection Intervention (2015). Poverty impacts or has the potential to result in each of the boxes in the middle, which in turn impacts the brain development of the child.

TRAUMA

One factor, which has been more frequently researched in recent years, is the impact of trauma on the brain. Trauma in early childhood and elementary grades can result in disrupted attachment, cognitive delays, and impaired emotional regulation. Also, the overdevelopment of certain pathways and the underdevelopment of other progressions can lead to impairment later in life (Perry, 1995).

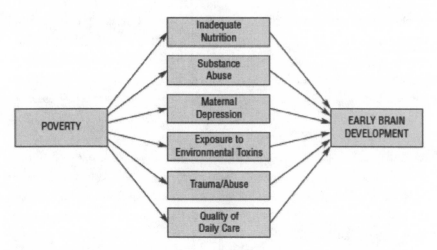

Figure 4.1 Brain Development in the Context of Poverty. *Source*: https://www.ok.gov/
health2/documents/Dr.%20Block%20-%20Social%20Detriments%20of%20Health.pdf.

For example, when a child experiences trauma for a majority of his/her/their
lifetime, the overdeveloped adrenal (fight-or-flight) instinct interacts with the
underdeveloped capacity to coping "appropriately." This also impacts sleeping, eating, thinking, and behavior. Therefore, it is imperative for educators
to understand that living in poverty is a traumatic experience that can have a
negative impact on the brain, which can explain a child's behavior, and how
we respond is important (see section "Challenging Behaviors").

Relationships and experiences teach the brain what to expect and how to
respond. When experiences are traumatic, the pathways getting the most use
are those that are in response to the trauma; this reduces the information of
other pathways needed for adaptive behavior. Trauma impacts the brain and
the aftereffects of trauma and stress can stay with someone for a lifetime,
especially children who experience severe trauma (The Center for Treatment
of Anxiety and Mood Disorders, 2017).

But what is trauma? The term "trauma" has various definitions; however,
it is, essentially, "a deeply distressing or disturbing experience" (SAMHSA-
HRSA, n.d.). It can be an experience that happens once (e.g., a tornado or
a house fire) or an enduring event (e.g., community violence or poverty).
Trauma can also include the absence of basic needs, such as safety and bonding (refer to Maslow's Hierarchy of Needs), which is a type of neglect. Overall, trauma not only impacts the "here and now" but also has the potential

to have a lifelong impact due to the high levels of stress impacting brain development and the lack of early access to quality schools, resulting in a disadvantage throughout one's lifetime (Boghani, 2017).

The two types of trauma that are often discussed are acute trauma and chronic trauma. Acute trauma is often one single life event, such as experiencing a natural disaster. Although it happens one time, it still can impact brain development and future interactions. Chronic trauma is trauma that is repetitive and lasts over a long period of time. Some examples of chronic trauma include experiencing and observing physical/sexual abuse, or experiencing ongoing neglect. Many acute traumas can result in chronic trauma. Additionally, referencing poverty, a middle-class family that experiences an acute trauma (i.e., tornado or the loss of a job in the family) could create the chronic trauma of long-term poverty (Poag, 2018).

Many times, trauma is associated with what is known as adverse childhood experiences (ACEs). ACEs are "experiences that harm children's developing brains and lead to changing how they respond to stress and damaging their immune systems so profoundly that the effects show up decades later" (aces-toohigh.com, n.d.). Overall, ACEs fall into three larger categories: childhood experiences, community experiences, and climate experiences. All of these can be impacted by poverty.

There is also another scale, which is not as well-known—the Juvenile Victimization Questionnaire (JVQ). The JVQ focuses on youth victimization ranging from conventional crime to maltreatment, to peer and sibling victimization, to sexual victimization, to witnessing violence. When using this scale victimization can be synonymous with trauma. In one research article, the authors used the JVQ to identify children who experienced poly-victimization (multiple victimizations). They found that 22 percent of children surveyed (total = 2,030 children) had experienced four or more different kinds of victimizations in the previous year. Overall, this questionnaire can help in identifying trauma/victimization in children (Finkelor, Ormrod, Turner, & Hamby, 2005).

One educator and researcher who was determined to find out more as a way to support her students reflected the following way:

> Ultimately I found that poverty DOES wire the brain differently. We had brain scans to prove it. I quickly decided that even though a brain on poverty over-wires its survival functions, (mammalian and reptilian) and under-wires our

prefrontal cortex, that didn't mean we were ignorant, or maladaptive or "less than." It meant we were brilliant! In fact, our brains had done a remarkable thing to adapt to the environments where the stakes were highest for survival. (Rebeca, 2019)

WHY IS POVERTY A TRAUMATIC EXPERIENCE?

"Nearly all possible consequences of poverty have an impact on children's' lives" (poverties.org, 2011). Growing up in poverty impacts everything in a child's life and brain development, from impulse control to anxiety (Collins, 2015). Furthermore, experts consider growing up poor as a kind of chronic, complex trauma. Jessica Trudeau, the director of development for the Momentous Institute (2015), stated, "[Trauma] can be living in poverty and the trauma that's associated with never having enough food for a child" (Collins, 2015).

Additionally, referring back to Maslow's Hierarchy of Needs, building attachment and social emotional well-being depends on receiving consistent love and trust from caregivers. Most often when a baby is born the parents feel an immediate and overwhelming sense of bonding. When this does not happen, potentially due to postpartum depression or hardships that come with poverty, it severely inhibits the child's ability to receive the love and trust needed to feel safe.

With poverty comes many potential obstacles to building healthy attachments. Parents may have to work multiple jobs, be stressed about money, be hungry, be scared, be exhausted, and so on. Under these conditions, children may experience neglect, be left alone, and lack the loving attachment they need to thrive. Lack of attachment is traumatic and, as trauma is, sustaining. "It was once believed that traumatic memories in the early days of life had no impact on the life of an individual. We now know that is not true" (Sorrels, 2015).

Poverty is a type of perpetual trauma that is experienced day in and day out. A child living in the perpetual trauma of poverty has a brain that is on constant "alert" or "fight-or-flight freeze." This constant brain state is then training the brain to be in that alert response constantly. This creates stress hormones, cortisol, to be released in the brain, creating a block to the prefrontal cortex, where the academic learning (impulse control, cause and effect, etc.)

are learned and mastered. "Physically, [children] feel the same kind of heart-pounding stress an adult feels after a car wreck. And they feel it all the time" due to the inconsistency of life (Collins, 2015). This feeling impacts the student's educational life because when hypervigilance is experienced, the constant fight, flight or freeze, the student is unable to go into the "learning mode," but rather stays in their "survival mode."

As Trudeau puts it, "If you think about the impact on education, imagine if right after you were in a car crash I walked up to you and said, 'I need you to take a test.' Could you do it? Would you perform well?" I know my answer would be "No."

POVERTY, TRAUMA, AND EDUCATION

Poverty is considered a traumatic, perpetual event in the life of a child. Poverty impacts the social and academic life of a student, and therefore impacts brain development. Overall, from the impact on the brain to the impact of daily life, poverty is often displayed in students through behaviors and reactions. While some students may show factors of resilience, other students may display challenging behaviors. As educators, it is our job to ensure that we are "seeing" all children for who they are, their capitals, and their backgrounds.

In addition, we must realize that for some students school is a safe haven, and the classroom may be the only consistently safe place in their lives. This may be evident in student behaviors as they may let their guard down, resulting in anything from a more relaxed body language to a need to sleep or rest or physical contact from a teacher such as frequent hugs. Older students may fall asleep on their desk or ask to visit the nurse often. Younger students may be clingy or want to always sit near the teacher. While teachers may see some of these behaviors as challenging, it is important to understand that they may signify that school is a safe space, and home is not.

Building strong relationships can help students develop coping strategies and feel a sense of security in the school environment. Important topics around the idea of developing coping strategies not only include the ideas surrounding challenging behaviors and qualities of resilience, which will be discussed later, but also include the strategy of self-regulation. Arguably self-regulation is an aspect of social emotional development that suffers the most when experiencing trauma, which results in challenging behaviors.

Self-regulation involves controlling one's emotions, behaviors, actions, and thoughts. In education self-regulation is often discussed in terms of emotional self-regulation, or the ability to manage personal emotions and impulses that may impact a classroom environment. Self-regulation skills are calming skills and coping skills, both of which can be taught through caring and mutually respectful relationships/interactions.

Being able to develop self-regulation skills benefits students living in poverty not only in the classroom but also in their unpredictable environments. It is stated that self-regulation "is a set of skills that enables children, as they mature, to direct their own behavior towards a goal, despite the unpredictability of the world and our own feelings" (Child Mind Institute, 2020).

Challenging Behaviors

Challenging behaviors have many definitions. However, in this section, this definition will be used: a culturally abnormal behavior that is so intense that personal safety or environmental safety (others' safety) is in danger. There are many types of challenging behaviors that are generally placed in the following categories:

1. cause injury to self or others
2. cause damage to the physical environment
3. interfere with learning new skills
4. socially isolate a student
5. are inappropriate for age or cultural background of student
6. are challenging for educators or family members to manage

As an educator it is important to understand that trauma does not define a child/student and it is not our job to fix the "problem." However, as educators understanding the child's background is the first step in addressing challenging behaviors. Understanding the concepts of brain development and the impact of trauma on brain development are part of this process. Additionally, the following two quotes are a good place to start the reflection process of difficult behaviors:

Challenging behaviors of traumatized children are driven by fear—not rebellion and defiance. (Sorrels, 2015)

Scared children do scary things because they are afraid and not because they are trying to get on the last nerve of the people who care for and teach them. (Sorrels, 2015)

Educators' first step needs to be understanding the "why" behind the behavior. Are there changes at home? Are there changes in the community? Is there trauma in the past or present? It is important to remember that challenging behaviors have a purpose. Another step, prior to the prevention plan, is to understand the function of the behavior in the classroom. Finally, it is imperative to form a strong, mutually respectful relationship with the student that is built in trust and unconditional love.

After the relationship has been built, understanding the form and function of the behavior is the next step. What is the behavior telling us? Remember, a student is not giving *us* a hard time, they are having a hard time. Thinking about the Antecedent, Behavior, and Consequence (ABCs) of the challenging behavior event can lead to teacher reflection and begin the process of action planning. The behavior is not always harmful or interruptive. Sometimes the behavior is going to the nurse's office frequently, complaining of a stomach-ache (anxiety), or blurting out in class as a way to gain attention.

Figure 4.2 shows a flowchart to help begin the process of understanding the student's life and background, as well as understanding how to address the challenging behavior, that is most likely linked to the trauma in the child's life. Because remember, a child's brain is not completely developed until their mid-twenties (prefrontal cortex) and the trauma of poverty impacts the development and connections occurring in this part of the brain.

Challenging Behavior Flow Chart

Reflection: What challenging behaviors do you see in your classroom? Reflect on the ABCs and see if you can "look past" the behavior and at the students' life/experiences.

Resilience

Resilience, as it was defined in chapter 3 as part of Resilience Theory, is the act of "bouncing back." According to the APA, resilience is the process of adapting well in the face of adversity, trauma, tragedy, threats, or even significant sources of risk or in other words, an effective means of coping.

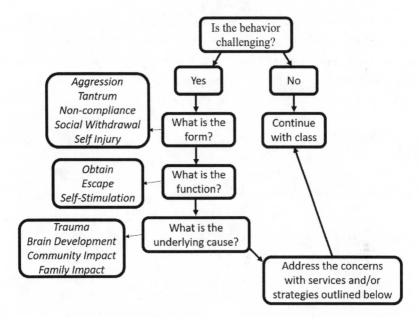

Figure 4.2   Challenging Behavior Flowchart. *Source*: Created by A. Reinking, 2019.

According to research, there are four main qualities associated with resilience (APA):

1. A positive view of oneself and confidence in one's strengths and abilities.
2. Skills in communication and problem-solving.
3. The capacity to make realistic plans and take steps to carry them out.
4. The ability to manage negative feelings and impulses.

One way children who live in poverty can flourish is through building relationships with consistent and trusting adults. While relationships are important, developing social emotional competence, which is the ability to manage emotions, express needs and feelings, deal with conflict, and get along with others, is a skill that will last a lifetime. Social emotional competence includes the developmentally appropriate coping skills of self-awareness, social awareness, self-management, relationship management, and responsible decision-making, most of which is developed and occurs in the prefrontal cortex of the brain.

These concepts support the work of Dr. Daniel Goleman, who focuses on social intelligence. According to Goleman, social intelligence has essentially four components: self-awareness and self-management, and social-awareness and social-skills. It is essentially the ability to successfully build relationships and navigate social environments. One idea from the work of Goleman is that "loneliness and weak relationships are one of the major sources of stress, health problems, and depression" (Science of People, 2019).

Social emotional competence has proven to be an important protective factor, buffering children from stressors and aiding in the prevention of serious emotional and behavioral difficulties, such as internalizing and externalizing behaviors (Wilson-Simmons, Jiang, & Aratani, 2017). Internalizing behaviors appear in the form of withdrawal, depression, anxiety, and fearfulness.

Shy and withdrawn behavior in reaction to social interaction may be among the first signs of internalizing problems in childhood. Researchers have found associations between children's internalizing behaviors and insecure parent-child attachment, often as a result of maternal depression. Supporting this idea, Kaiser, Li, Pollmann-Schult, and Song (2017) found that the impact of poverty as trauma decreased as material life satisfaction increased.

Externalizing behaviors include inattention, impulsivity, and aggression. Once these problems become established behaviors in children, they tend to be chronic, placing children at high risk for a range of negative outcomes such as academic failure; rejection by peers; poor relationships with siblings, peers, parents, and other adults; and delinquency (Caspi & Moffitt, 1995; Pitzer, Esser, Schmidt, & Laucht, 2009).

Both externalizing and internalizing behaviors do not lead to resilient characteristics. However, research has shown that when caregivers have knowledge of what their child is doing during their free time, have knowledge of friendships, spend time with their children, listen to their child, and talk over larger important decisions, social emotional competence is more developed and can overcome some of the hardships associated with the trauma of poverty.

Reflection: What externalizing and internalizing behaviors do you see in your students? How will having this knowledge positively impact your work in the classroom?

Students who are experiencing or who have experienced trauma, specifically poverty as trauma, may display challenging behaviors, adverse academic outcomes, and physical health problems. But why? Most of the impact stems from the research focused on the impact of trauma on brain development.

An overview of the negative effects of children living in poverty is outlined by the APA (APA, 2019). In the APA report, it is evident that poverty impacts students' lives in all facets, from home to school to neighborhoods, to communities. The APA states that "poverty is linked with negative conditions such as substandard housing, homelessness, inadequate nutrition and food insecurity, inadequate child-care, lack of access to health care, unsafe neighborhoods, and under resourced schools" (2019).

Under-resourced schools are one of the leading factors in the opportunity gap between students who live in communities with money and resources and those that do not. Under-resourced schools adversely impact students due to unsafe environments, outdated materials, and a sense of "we don't matter." Additionally, students who live in poverty have adverse effects in their academic outcomes due to chronic stress, which impedes their learning, concentration, and memory (refer to "Brain Development").

Students living in poverty also are "at a greater risk of behavioral and emotional problems" (APA, 2019), or challenging behaviors. One group of researchers stated, "The detrimental impact of poverty on child behavioral problems is well-established" (Kaiser, Li, Pollmann-Schult, & Song, 2017). Due to stress hormones, constant fight or flight, and a feeling of insecurity, students living in poverty are at a higher risk to show behaviors of impulsivity, arguments with peers, aggressive behaviors, and conduct disorders. Many of these challenging behaviors stem from a lack of brain development and the emotional feelings of anxiety, depression, and low self-esteem.

Anxiety, depression, and low self-esteem, as a result of the trauma of poverty, can also lead to physical health problems. It has been found that "children and teens living in poorer communities are at increased risk for a wide range of physical health problems" (APA, 2019). There are many causes for the physical health problems from lack of access to healthy foods (food deserts), lack of access to areas for physical activity, and lack of access to safe neighborhood and communities, which creates exposure to violence leading to possible injury, disability, or mortality.

Additionally, students living in poverty often experience environmental poverty, which can lead to asthma, anemia, and pneumonia, as well as chronic infections. Moreover, children living in poverty have a greater risk of being exposed to environmental contaminants such as lead paint and toxic waste.

Another example of environmental poverty focus on high rates of cancer among communities of people living in impoverished areas. As stated by researchers Heidary, Rahimi, and Gharebaghi (2013), "Poverty remains one of the most potent carcinogens . . . poverty is the initial contributing factor to cancer disparities among social groups, and that racial differences in biological or inherited characteristics are less significant. The fact is that people living in poverty lack access to health care and subsequently endure greater pain and illness" (para. 4).

All of these factors or effects are compounded by the barriers children and their families encounter when trying to access physical and mental health care. Overall, poorer students are also at greater risk for "poor academic achievement, school dropout, abuse and neglect, behavioral and socioemotional problems, physical health problems, and developmental delays" (2019).

Chapter 5

Homelessness

It's hard. You can't sleep. . . . And your stomach hurts, and you're thinking 'I can't sleep. I'm going to try and sleep, I'm going to try and sleep' but you can't cause your stomach's hurting. And it's 'cause it doesn't have any food in it.

(Student on CBS's 60 Minutes
focused on Homelessness)

As of 2019, it was reported that 2.5 million children are homeless each year in America, which equates to one in every thirty children in the United States (American Institutes for Research, 2019). Furthermore, "children are homeless in every city, county, and state throughout our country" (American Institutes for Research, 2019). Of those homeless children, 87 percent reported they worry something bad will happen to their families. However, it is important to state that every family living in poverty does not experience homelessness, but homelessness is often discussed in association with poverty.

Reflection: Before reading on, take a few minutes to think or write down your definition of homelessness. What is homelessness? What do you see when you see a homeless family?

WHAT IS HOMELESSNESS?

While some people may define it as "the state of having no home," the Oxford Encyclopedia of Social Work defines homelessness as a person who "lacks a fixed, regular, and adequate nighttime residence, and if they sleep in a shelter designated for temporary living accommodations or in places not designated for human habitation" (Law Hawaii, 2018). From this definition, there are also outliers, which are included in the high statistics of homelessness in America. Homelessness also includes the following:

- "Doubled up" or the concept of couch surfing (i.e., staying with friends and family). Doubled up occurs when the individual staying in the living area is not on the lease or mortgage.
- Precariously housed or the concept where members would become homeless in less than three months if they suddenly lost their primary source of income.
- Hidden homeless or the concept where more than one family share accommodations. These households include families that are doubled up (two or more families or groups of persons who are related by birth, marriage, or adoption) and those that are sharing (two or more families or groups whose members are not related by birth, marriage, or adoption).

Additionally, the Salvation Army, who is often one of the social service agencies in communities that provides support and service to homeless individuals and families, states homelessness as not having suitable accommodations and the current shelter/dwelling is inadequate, short-term, or does not allow control and access to space for social relationships (Salvation Army, 2019). Remember, just because a child or family has shelter does not mean that it is a safe shelter.

TYPES OF HOMELESSNESS

While that is the inclusive definition of homelessness, there are also four types of homelessness. What is important to remember is that homelessness does not always look like someone sleeping on the streets, but rather it can take many forms. The four categories of homelessness that we will focus on are chronic, episodic, transitional, and hidden.

If an individual is homeless for a year or more, regardless of ability, the individual or family is considered to be living in chronic homelessness (Jaggi, 2019). Additionally, if an individual or family has experienced episodic homelessness (defined later) for a minimum of four episodes over three years, they are also considered to be chronically homeless.

The most common type of homelessness is transitional homelessness. Statistics state that individuals experiencing transitional homelessness are "younger and generally enter a shelter or temporary housing system" (Jaggi, 2019). While transitional homelessness can be the result of a variety of life events, often transitional homeless individuals experienced a catastrophic event or sudden life change that has impacted shelter and economic stability.

Episodic homelessness is when an individual or family has experienced homelessness during periods of time over a twelve-month period. Generally, to be classified as episodic homeless, individuals or families would experience three episodes in a twelve-month time period, with the wider definition of what it means to be homeless. Again, often episodic homelessness is experienced by a younger population or individuals who have an addiction or mental illness (Jaggi, 2019).

The final type of homelessness that is often defined by researchers and individuals who work with homeless individuals is known as hidden homelessness. Individuals who fall into this category of homelessness often do not access support or services provided by the community to homeless individuals, despite their needs. Therefore, as the word states, this type of homelessness is hidden and therefore often unreported. Another term for individuals experiencing hidden homelessness is known as "provisionally occupied" or "temporary living with others (i.e. couch surfing) without a guarantee that they will be able to stay long-term and without immediate prospects for acquiring permanent housing" (Jaggi, 2019).

Homelessness, as defined by the Salvation Army (2019), can be a result of several events in an individual or family's life. However, the events that occur most often to result in homelessness include poverty, unemployment, lack of affordable housing, poor physical or mental health, drug or alcohol abuse, gambling, family and relationship breakdowns, or domestic violence. Additionally, youth who experience homelessness (i.e., teenagers) are often in the LGBTQ+ community and do not feel safe and/or accepted at home. According to a 2017 report on homelessness, LGBTQ+ youth account for up to 40 percent of homeless youth (Chapin Hall at the University of Chicago, 2017). The Human Rights Campaign (HRC) confirms these findings, which show that "LGBTQ young adults had a 120 percent higher risk of reporting homelessness compared to youth who identified as heterosexual and cisgender," are consistent with other research. HRC (2020) states,

> LGBTQ youth aren't the only population that disproportionately experience homelessness, according to the data released today. Other young adult populations experiencing disproportionate rates of homelessness include Black and African American youth, Hispanic non-white youth, unmarried parenting youth, youth with less than a high school diploma or GED certificate and youth reporting annual household income of less than $24,000.

Reflection: What are your experiences with LGBTQ+ youth and homelessness? Sometimes supporting youth to come out to their families can result in homelessness. What are some steps you can take when supporting LGBTQ+ students and what are some precautions? (For more information visit the HRC website.)

It is also important to see homelessness from the view of Maslow's Hierarchy of Needs, especially when viewing homeless through the eyes of students. As a reminder, Maslow's Hierarchy of Needs supports the concept "individuals must satisfy lower level deficit needs before progressing on to meet higher level growth need" (McLeod, 2018). The lower level needs include air, water, food, shelter, sleep, clothing, personal security, and health, to name a few. These lower level, yet foundational, needs are often impacted by poverty and/or homelessness.

Reflection: What are your experiences with school transience? Have you had students move into your classroom midyear or move into town over the summer? How did you support them?—Did you learn about where they attended last? How did you help them to feel a sense of belonging in your classroom?

Homelessness and living in poverty can also lead to school transience. School transience or school mobility "is any time a student changes school for reasons other than grade promotion, but in general it refers to students changing schools during a school year" (Sparks, 2016). While families who are not homeless or do not experience poverty may move often, such as military families, there are many reasons why families living in poverty move often (e.g., evictions, housing discrimination, gentrification, job loss, etc.) resulting in a high rate of school transience. It has been found that when students are already experiencing factors in their life that impact their learning, moving often is harmful.

A professor at University of California, Santa Barbara, Russell Rumberger, found "multiple moves are a dangerous signal, but even one move increases the [student's] risk of not graduating or getting delayed in graduating." The statistics state, children who are homeless move 50 percent to 100 percent more than their middle-class peers, which results in frequent school changes. These frequent school changes create instability in the students' educational career, which results in lower academic achievement.

Furthermore, "a 2010 Government Accountability Office study followed students who entered kindergarten in 1998 through 2007. It found 13 percent of students changed schools four or more times by the end of 8th grade, and highly mobile students were disproportionately more likely to be poor or black than students who changed schools twice or fewer times" (Sparks, 2015). In addition to the transient mobility of families living in poverty is the increased stress of eviction, bills, moving costs, and police interactions.

Regardless of the family or student's living situation, it is important to remember that homelessness does not define a person but is instead a temporary situation. There is no single face or cause of homelessness (Homeless Connections, 2019). However, instability can have lasting consequences for children. Along these lines, one important thing for schools and teachers to consider is how we can increase communication when students move from school to school.

Often it may not be possible to find out where the student last attended. However, when that information is provided, it is important to contact the last teacher to learn about the student's strengths, weaknesses, and experiences. Furthermore, it is also important to keep in mind that we may not even know when a student is homeless. Families may want to keep it secret, and even tell the student to not share their circumstance.

While knowing the experiences of students is important, it is also important to understand how language can impact an inclusive classroom environment. For example, often in classrooms teachers and/or students will talk about or ask the question, "Where do you live or who do you live with?" For a student experiencing homelessness this is often difficult to answer. A middle-class peer may answer, "I live with my family in our house down the street." However, homeless students often will use the word "stay" rather than "live" and will not use the word "home." Therefore, engaging in these conversations in class "out" a student as homeless, which may be embarrassing or traumatizing for the students. As educators we can have more inclusive conversations such as, "Who do you spend time with?"

Reflection: What are the signs that one of your students may be experiencing homelessness? If you suspect this is true, what would you do? How might you support that student?

MCKINNEY VENTO ACT

Knowing that homelessness does not discriminate, or anyone can experience homelessness depending on life situations, the U.S. Department of Education passed the Education for Homeless Children and Youths, also known as the McKinney-Vento Homeless Assistance Act (2001). This legislation defines homeless children and youth as "individuals who lack a fixed, regular, and adequate nighttime residence" which includes sharing housing, living in motels, living on campgrounds, or living in emergency or transitional housing. Additionally, it includes children or youth abandoned in hospitals, a nighttime residence that was not designed for human being accommodations including cards, parks, public spaces, abandoned buildings, or bus/train stations.

Furthermore, migratory children, with a designated definition, are also considered homeless under the McKinney-Vento Act. In simplistic terms, "The McKinney-Vento Act is a federal law that ensures the right of students to go to school even when they are homeless or don't have a permanent address. The Act aims to reduce barriers that have prevented many homeless youth from enrolling, attending, and succeeding in school" (RHYIssues@aGlance, 2012). Another school requirement as outlined by the Act is that every school district has to have a homeless education liaison who works with young people, schools, and service providers to make sure that transition is smoother and the needed support are provided.

Once a school district determines a student's homelessness status, as defined by the Act, the McKinney-Vento Act regulates the urgently needed assistance to protect and improve the lives and safety of the homeless. The assistance school districts provide for children and youth focus on protecting their rights to go to school. Specifically, the Act states that schools need to reduce the barriers of transportation and requirements such as residency within a district and needed documentation that may be more difficult to acquire, such as birth certificates and/or medical records. Eradicating these barriers, students who are supported under the McKinney-Vento Act can go to the school that is nearest to their current location or where they were last enrolled, even if they moved out of the district. In this case, the district must provide transportation.

Reflection: Does your school district have a homeless education liaison? To whom might you go in your district for support if you discover you have a student who is homeless?

ACADEMIC ACHIEVEMENT

Academic achievement is impacted by homelessness, similarly to the impact of poverty in the life of a student. Imagine a five-year-old child or a ten-year-old child or a fifteen-year-old child who is hungry, did not get even two hours of sleep the night before, and does not know where they are going at the end of the school day. You as an educator are standing in front of them talking about colors, or fractions, or geography expecting their brains to work and be awake.

Now, as an adult put yourself in that situation. Imagine being hungry, exhausted, and having the stress of not knowing where you will go or if you will have a safe place to sleep when it gets dark outside. Imagine how much concentration you would have in that situation and then your boss walks up to you and expects you to have a lengthy, two-hour conversation about a brand-new project, or assessment strategy, or analyze data. Be honest. It would be difficult to impossible to concentrate. That is the same thing with our students who experience poverty and homelessness.

Figure 5.1 depicts the indicators of homelessness. These are behaviors to look for as an educator when interacting with the students in your classroom (Firth, 2019).

It is important to know that the impact of homelessness does not start when a child is five, truly it begins prenatally. However, children birth to five years old statistically experience a deficit in vocabulary and sentence development based on hearing fewer words in their environment and the language that is heard is based on a more concrete and literal meaning, rather than being abstract adjective rich. Researchers at Stanford University released a study called the 30 Million Word Gap which tracked the achievement gap back to

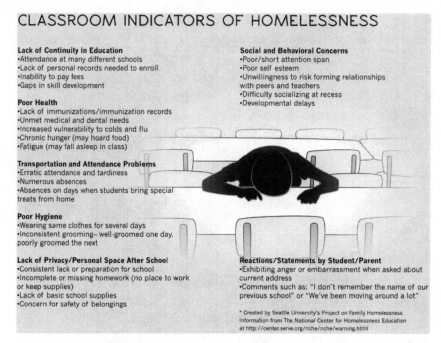

Figure 5.1 Classroom Indicators of Homelessness. *Source*: Created by Seattle University's Project on Family Homelessness information from The National Center for Homelessness Education at http://center.serve.org/nche/nche/warning.html.

eighteen months, where children who live in poverty have millions of fewer words in their vocabulary than their more affluent peers.

A great deal of research has supported the role of oral language on written language development. Oral language is the foundation for written language. When students begin kindergarten with limited language they are already behind and have a much more difficult time learning to read. In addition, students living in poverty often have less exposure to books and other concepts about print, both very important in reading and writing acquisition.

Aside from these deficits and their implications, preschoolers who experience homelessness had less motor-visual abilities; had more emotional-behavioral challenges, such as impulsivity or lack of emotional regulation, in the classroom; and have a higher rate of speech delays. Relating back to the information we learned about trauma, however, this makes sense as we consider toxic stress and traumatic experiences impacting the brain.

The developmental delays that are a result of environment and experiences slow a students' ability to progress to new ages of development, both academic and social. This often displays itself in a multitude of ways as the student progresses through their educational journey, as the rigor increases. The statistics support this concept.

In the 2011–2012 school year, 51 percent of homeless students met state-wide standards in reading in grades 3–8 and 48 percent met the standards in math. A major reason why students living in poverty struggle academically is the potential lack of prior knowledge they bring to school. Jean Piaget helped us to see the critical role that prior knowledge, or schema, plays in learning. Piaget believed learning is a connection between the known and the new. He believed we use our prior knowledge to make connections to understand the new information.

Prior knowledge is critical in reading and is directly correlated to vocabulary. When students have a caregiver who talks through daily hands-on experiences with them and provides critical content vocabulary, those students have developed schema that they can use when reading books in school, writing about various subjects or learning about science concepts. These daily experiences could be walks through the neighborhood or woods, museums, discussing everyday occurrences such as the mechanics of the bus or subway, how the gas pump or the postal system works, names of animals, and so on. It is difficult to read about or understand something about which you have little prior knowledge and when children come to school with a variety of experiences/prior knowledge, they are better poised for academic success.

Reflection: How do you assess student prior knowledge before starting a unit or reading a book? What can you do to activate and/or build the needed prior knowledge before starting that unit or book? What are some ways you can help your students to develop prior knowledge or take the prior knowledge they do have to direct your instruction? This is even more important for English language learners (ELLs). How can you assess and build the prior knowledge of your students who are ELLs?

Additionally, special education services needs to be discussed in relation with students who are homeless or living in poverty. Children experiencing poverty or homelessness are statistically more likely to end up receiving services. However, schools have reported significant challenges or roadblocks during the evaluation process. Some of the roadblocks include the lack of stability resulting in a loss of school records and the process of ruling out environmental causes (i.e., poverty or homelessness) impacting the students'

SIMILARITIES BETWEEN CLASSROOM INDICATORS OF ADHD AND HOMELESSNESS

(Some) Indicators of Homelessness	(Some) Indicators of ADHD	Points of Overlap
·Poor organizational skills ·Poor ability to conceptualize ·Mistaken diagnosis of abilities ·Consistent lack of preparation for school ·Incomplete or missing homework (no place to work or keep supplies) ·Loss of books and other supplies on a regular basis ·Poor/short attention span ·Poor self esteem ·Aggression ·Difficulty socializing at recess ·Fatigue	·Has difficulty planning, organizing, and completing tasks on time ·Inattention ·Has difficulty concentrating ·Has unrelated thoughts ·Appears to not be listening ·Has problems learning new things ·Demonstrates poor self-regulation of behavior, that is, he or she has difficulty monitoring and modifying behavior to fit different situations and settings	·Poor organizational and planning skills (so incomplete or missing homework) ·Fatigue can look like: problems concentrating and learning new things, not regulating behavior, not paying attention/listening ·Social problems ·Not completing tasks/homework on time ·Inattention

Created by Seattle University's Project on Family Homelessness
Sources:
National Center for Homeless Education
http://bit.ly/1u4Q87i
American Speech-Language-Hearing Association
http://bit.ly/Z97p3W

Figure 5.2   Similarities between Classroom Indicators of ADHD and Homelessness.

academic or social challenges. Figure 5.2 is an example of how homeless and Attention Deficit Hyperactivity Disorder (ADHD) have many similarities. This demonstrates just one example of the difficulty in the evaluation process (firesteelwa.org, 2019).

After the evaluation process, if it is determined that the student does have special education needs, the next barrier is accessing the services. Some barriers include the high rate of mobility, which can result in inconsistent services or unnoticed needs due to new schools/educators in their lives. The high mobility rate also can result in a loss of school records or discontinued services, which is directly linked to the high student mobility.

If a homeless student is evaluated and does receive services, the most common category of special education for homeless students is known as "emotional disturbance." This category of special education services that many students living in poverty or who are homeless receive is in direct relationship to the toxic stress and trauma impact in their lives (chapter 4).

The following are the characteristics of "emotional disturbance":

- An inability to learn that cannot be explained by intellectual, sensory, or health factors.
- An inability to build or maintain satisfactory interpersonal relationships with peers and teachers.
- An appropriate type of behavior or feelings under normal circumstances.
- A general pervasive mood of unhappiness or depression.
- A tendency to develop physical symptoms or fears associated with personal or school problems.

To be officially categorized with an "emotional disturbance" the one or more of the above characteristics have to be displayed over a long period of time and adversely impact a student's educational performance. While we can critically look at this category, it does not diminish the fact that students do need services to help with academic and social success.

CONCLUSIONS

As educators, it is our job to see the students for who they are and the experiences they have had, however, do not let those experiences define them. Rather, let those experiences impact how we facilitate learning with that student. When we consider the impact and develop strategies to facilitate learning, it is important to know more statistics or concepts that homeless children often experience.

First, children who are born to mothers who are homeless have low birth weights and require specialized care four times the rate of non-homeless peers (firesteelwa.org). This represents a disadvantaged start to life. Additionally, homeless (and poor) children are less likely to eat nutrient-rich food or go hungry. Both of these situations result in lower academic achievement. This also results in more stress on the body creating the statistic that homeless children are sick four times more than other children with respiratory infections, ear infections, gastro-intestinal problems, and asthma (National Center on Family Homelessness).

Educators can make a difference. Even just one caring, dedicated, proactive adult can change the life trajectory of a student. In future chapters we will discuss how teachers can create safe and productive learning environments where they intentionally plan and deliver student-centered lessons and build positive relationships with all students and their families.

Chapter 6

Economic Shaming, Food Shaming, Behavior Shaming

*On the morning bus, kids are laughing and talking about what they did
on the weekend, except Bob. He is looking down at his feet, noticing the
new rip along the seam of his right sneaker. He would like a new pair
of sneakers, which would be the first new pair he has even worn, but
right now what he would like even more is to go the whole day without
anyone else noticing, especially Samantha. Last week she teased him
for having a rip in his shirt. In fact, he thought, she teases him about
his clothes all the time.*

School can be a difficult place for children living in poverty, a place that often
feels far from safe due to daily micro- and macroaggressions from peers and
adults alike. A microaggression is an act of discrimination toward an individual (e.g., "Did you finally get some new clothes?") and a macroaggression
is an act of discrimination toward an entire group of people (e.g., "Maybe if
people worked harder they would have more money."). Children and families
who live in poverty are subjected to this implicit and explicit discrimination
in schools on a daily basis. As a result, they are often left feeling an intense
sense of shame. In this chapter we will discuss three major areas of shaming
that pervasively occur in the classroom, on the bus, in the cafeteria, at school
events, and so on. These are economic shaming, food shaming, and behavior shaming. But first, we will discuss the painful and debilitating nature of
shame.

SHAME AND VULNERABILITY

Before breaking down the types of shaming that children and families in poverty experience, we need to first examine shame. The social scientist and research professor Brene Brown has spent over twenty years researching shame and vulnerability. On her website she defines shame as "the intensely painful feeling or experience of believing that we are flawed and therefore unworthy of love and belonging—something we've experienced, done, or failed to do makes us unworthy of connection." She then goes on to say, "I don't believe shame is helpful or productive. In fact, I think shame is much more likely to be the source of destructive, hurtful behavior than the solution or cure. I think the fear of disconnection can make us dangerous."

Sadly, children and families living in poverty face the challenges of shame on a daily basis simply because of their SES. Recall Maslow who theorized that there is a hierarchy of our basic human needs, and the needs at the bottom of that hierarchy (air, water, sleep, food, shelter, clothing, safety, love) must be met before we are able to move up to ultimately being self-actualized beings.

Many educational philosophies have been based entirely on this humanistic theory. Maria Montessori, for instance, based her philosophy of teaching and learning from grades pre-K to 12 on humanistic beliefs. Her original research was on children living in extreme poverty and while no one else at the time believed the children were capable of learning, Montessori proved that if their basic human needs were met, they could learn.

As Brene Brown points out, not only does shame create an intense lack of the very things children and families living in poverty need the most from their school community, which is safety, love, and belonging, but it also perpetuates their belief that they are flawed and unworthy. It would be difficult for anyone to achieve academic success under these conditions. Without their basic human needs being met, there is far from a level playing field between children living in poverty and their more affluent peers. As a result, children who live in poverty experience the devastating effects of shame on a daily basis.

ECONOMIC SHAMING

There are numerous ways in which economic shaming plays out for children and families living in poverty. Economic shaming refers to the family's inability to meet the financial expectations of a school. For instance, families living in poverty often cannot meet the monetary contributions or requirements they are asked to pay. On a regular basis families are asked for money for school supplies, lunch or classroom snacks, field trips, class parties, projects, and so on. Even though a single financial contribution (e.g., $2.00 each toward class snack) may seem small, for families in poverty that small contribution, if paid at all, may come directly out of the week's grocery money.

However, paying the money may be better than sending a child to school who is the only one who cannot contribute to class snack. In this way we are putting children and families between a rock and a hard place—either send in money we do not have or experience the shame of not doing so. Further, these small amounts add up, and fast. While this is a reality for many families in the United States, the majority of teachers are middle class, creating a potential insensitivity as it is hard for them to imagine that sending in such a small amount could be extremely difficult for a family living in poverty.

A colleague, Ms. Laycee Thigpen, reported the following experience to Dr. Reinking while writing this book:

I was attending my son's school's PTO meeting and the President was presenting our yearly budget and was explaining how much money the PTO spends on purchasing snacks for classroom parties. It was then suggested that each student brings in $2 and that will be used to cover the cost of the snack instead of PTO paying for it. The overall consensus was that it was a good idea.

I sat there and remained silent. When my son started school, he qualified for free lunch because of our family's low income. I was a stay-at-home mom at the beginning of school but had recently started working a new job. I kept thinking about the $2 each child was going to be asked to provide to enjoy their classroom party.

After the meeting, I spoke with the PTO president and I asked, "Is it mandatory for the children to bring the $2?" "I think some parents will be willing to donate snacks for the entire class." She and the other committee members reassured me that if the child does not bring the money then they can still participate in the party. I began to explain to them that I am glad because I do not want any child to be left out because they do not have $2.

I still left feeling disheartened because I know some parents will feel obligated to send money in with their child. Regardless if they do not have it, they will "figure it out" just so that their child does not look like "the poor kid." That $2 may be gas money, grocery money, emergency fund money, but my son's school's PTO were asking parents to use it for a holiday party snack.

Financially supporting the school in various events and donations are not the only type of economic shaming. Another area of economic shaming relates to clothes shaming. Children who live in poverty are often singled out, teased, and bullied simply because of the clothes they wear to school. Not only are these children not able to keep up with fads and styles, they often are also wearing clothes that are hand-me-downs, either from older siblings or secondhand shops. As a result, their clothes may be too small or too big, ripped or stained. Washing clothes, an added expense, may be difficult for families and children may wear the same clothes to school for multiple days in a row, resulting in smelly or visibly dirty clothes.

Another experience of clothing shaming relates to having enough or appropriate clothing for the weather or class activities. For instance, in the winter they may not be able to go out for recess if they don't have warm coats or boots. Physical education and field trips are also often problematic since it is necessary to have sneakers in the gym or appropriate clothing to participate in extracurricular activities.

The peer pressure to wear "acceptable" clothing can be so intense that some children and families go to extreme lengths to get that certain pair of sneakers or name brand clothing. Children may steal and parents may sacrifice money that would be best used for food or bills to succumb to the pressure of clothing shaming. It is fair to say that next to the color of our skin, the clothing we wear may be one of the first thing people notice about us.

School supplies, backpacks, items from home for sharing time, technology, books, and so on are also of concern. Children may need to bring their books to school in a plastic bag or consistently need writing utensils or not have a smartphone to look up the information a teacher asks for, or a calculator for math, and so on. Economic shaming does not just relate to the children, but their family members, as well. Children may not want their peers to see the car their caregiver drives up in, or the clothing they are wearing, or the house they live in as the bus pulls up. There are many ways in which children living in poverty may experience the feeling of shame about their family members. This is extremely difficult as it perpetuates even more shame because they may feel badly that they were ashamed of the people they love. These are just a few of the many ways that children living in poverty regularly experience economic shaming in school.

Reflection: After reading this, what are some ways students in your school might be experiencing economic shaming? If so, what are strategies you could do to diminish the practice?

FOOD SHAMING

An extension of economic shaming but worthy of its own category is food shaming. Food is such a big part of our school day, and our lives. There are many ways that children and families living in poverty experience food shaming. Food shaming could happen during snack or lunchtime, on field trips, and on special events like field days. Both children and families experience food shaming over the school year.

A caregiver may be judged by the classroom teacher for sending in food that is not of high quality or is lacking in quantity, or maybe the dish appears to be old or dirty. This could be for their child, or their contribution to a class snack or party. Sometimes children are told they could approach the teacher's desk for a snack if they don't have one in which case children who never have a snack face the dilemma of approaching the teacher's desk on the daily or going hungry. Other times children are told they can go to the nurse to get a snack and many times they simply have to go without and are hungry.

A big aspect of food shaming relates to free or reduced lunch. The National School Lunch Program was created in 1946 and since then it has been widely used to measure poverty levels in schools and districts. It has been estimated that nearly 30 million children receive free or reduced lunch in the United States. These children are widely underfed, rarely have the freedom to choose what they eat, are often recognized by their poverty level, and certainly have a difficult time achieving status, self-esteem, and a sense of safety.

When children receive free or reduced lunch, they certainly are at risk of food shaming, and not only by their peers. In fact, there have been many examples of administrators shaming children and their families. In 2019, a

Pennsylvania administrator threatened to report families to social services if they didn't pay their school lunch debt. In some schools, children who receive free/reduced lunch are not able to choose from the available selection but have to have a certain designated meal such as P&J sandwiches. Some schools stamp children's hand if they need a free lunch, and others have refused giving lunches to children because they have unpaid accounts of less than $10.00. And then there are the millions of children who don't qualify for free lunch, but don't have enough food to eat, or have no food at all. School lunch shaming is well-documented and has received national attention.

The National School Lunch Program has had numerous problems since its inception. The much-needed change in policies and procedures has become even more important recently since the current administration has proposed to make severe enough cuts to the Supplemental Nutrition Assistance Program to negatively impact more than one million children and families.

An additional concept that often impacts families/students experiencing food shaming, which also relates to community poverty, is the concept of a food desert. A food desert is an area or community that has limited to no access to affordable and nutritious food. This contrasts food oases, which are communities or areas that have access to supermarkets with fresh food. Generally, in food deserts families and community members have limited access to food within walking distance, such as corner stores or gas stations. This lack of nutritious choices within walking distance of a neighborhood creates families and students who have poor diets and rely on gas stations for a majority of their household food items.

Reflection: After reading this, what are some way students in your school might be experiencing food shaming? If so, what are the strategies you could do to diminish the practice?

BEHAVIOR SHAMING

While the term "hangry" has received recent attention, *Merriam-Webster* tracked it back to 1918 and defines it as "irritable or angry because of hunger." We have all been there. Extended hunger makes us feel frustrated, impatient, and outright angry. While there may not be a clever and popular portmanteau for all of the other basic human needs (e.g., water, sleep, safety, security of family, love and a home, etc.), the absence of them has the exact same effect. Bottom line, it is difficult and close to impossible to be able to learn or of best behavior when we are hungry, scared, insecure, unsafe, thirsty, tired, and more.

In fact, when we are feeling even just one of these it is easy to imagine exhibiting aggression, tantrums, and other noncompliant behaviors. Yet, often the child is to blame and children who lack these basic needs are seen as having "behavior problems" themselves, or in the least, seen as difficult. The macroaggression here may be "He is just trying to get attention." or "She is just trying to get out of taking the test."

As a result, children and their families experience severe behavior shaming. When the challenging behaviors are seen as a problem with the child, they may be subjected to numerous isolating, embarrassing, and near abusive classroom practices, or microaggressions. For example, the child's desk may be moved away from a group and isolated somewhere since he is "unable to behave in a group." Maybe a behavior modification program is set up for that child and as a consequence she misses recess often. Or even worse, a whole class behavior modification program is put in place and the child is responsible for the whole class losing a marble, resulting in a loss of recess time for everyone.

These practices create negative exchanges between children, and before long the child feels ostracized by the class. Recall how Brene Brown says, "I think the fear of disconnection can make us dangerous." Often children and families living in poverty feel disconnected from the school community.

If the behavior is seen to be a problem within the child, and not the circumstance, family members are also blamed and seen as responsible for their child's challenging behavior. The macroaggression here may be "If you made sure your child got more sleep, or was more respectful of adults, or you disciplined your child better at home, and so on, he wouldn't be behaving this way." Family members may receive many phone calls with negative feedback about their child, be called in to school for conferences with a whole team of school personnel, or be told their child may receive a suspension or even be expelled.

There are numerous ways in which children and families living in poverty are behavior shamed. If we could all think back to a time where we were hangry, or exhausted, or scared, it is easy to see the challenging behavior for what it is, the result of an intense lack of a basic human need. When we blame the child and family it creates a cyclical pattern of negative behaviors that is close to impossible to reverse.

When we address the behavior with an openness and willingness to identify the culprit, we listen and learn from the family and child and all work together to identify the need and provide the solution. Sometimes this could be something amazingly simple such as providing breakfast first thing on a Monday when a child may return to school after a weekend of hunger, or a nap in the nurse's office after a night with little sleep due to extreme noise in the apartment building, or a walk outside where the fresh air and exercise is calming and sets the stage for classroom integration. If we don't work to learn about what is prompting the behavior, we will never find the solution.

Reflection: After reading this, are there ways students in your school experience behavior shaming? If so, what are strategies you could do to diminish the practice?

CONCLUSIONS

While it may simply be impossible to eradicate the shaming that some children and families experience regularly, there are many things that can be done to minimize it and create safer school/classroom climates. As is the case with all areas of successful culturally responsive teaching, all school personnel (teachers, paraprofessionals, bus drivers, administrators, board members) need to become aware of the myriad of ways children and families living in poverty experience shaming in schools. These individuals must take this heightened awareness and sensitivity and modify school/town policies and protocol.

Town/school initiatives such as free or reduced breakfast and lunch, as well as extracurricular school-wide expectations such as field trips or other expenses expected of families, must go through the same scrutiny. Teachers should be given opportunities to discuss their experiences and concerns regarding the shaming of children and families living in poverty. Teachers can then work together to reflect on ways to modify their classroom practices and minimize those experiences as much as possible.

This could include small changes from not asking children to walk to the teacher's desk if they need a snack, to using children's books and social studies curricula to have explicit discussions with children regarding the micro- and macroaggressions children and families living in poverty experience—the most difficult conversations are the most important and teachers must feel safe and comfortable enough to have these conversations with the class, and their families.

This heightened awareness, sensitivity, and empathy are critical to minimizing our students' participation in such aggressions, and supporting them to be allies, over bystanders. Perhaps most important is helping students feel empowered and view themselves as change agents. Class and school fundraisers and participating in community efforts can help students to see that their relatively small efforts can make a big difference in the lives of others. Ultimately, we need to remember these words from Brene Brown and do everything we can to prevent our children and families from experiencing shame: "I don't believe shame is helpful or productive. In fact, I think shame is much more likely to be the source of destructive, hurtful behavior than the solution or cure."

Chapter 7

The Importance of Building Positive Relationships and School Climates

They don't care how much you know until they know how much you care

—John C. Maxwell

The kids who need the most love will ask for it in the most unloving ways

—Russell Barkley

Relationships are the foundation for trust, respect, and growth. Educators who are able to build strong relationships with students understand the foundation of student needs: safety and love. While building strong relationships may not be easy, it very well may be the single most important thing you can do as a student's teacher; it is the basis for everything you do. Though this is true for all students, students who live in poverty need this trusting and caring respectful relationship even more. In fact and as discussed in chapter 5, for many children school is the only safe place in their lives, the place where they can let their guard down and breathe more deeply, the place that makes the most sense. These students may have not had many relationships built on trust and consistency, and as such, they may have learned to mistrust their environment and the people in it. This could create an uphill battle for you as their teacher, and there are specific strategies that can help.

While there are many ways to develop strong relationships between teachers and students, we will focus on four: 2 × 10 (2 by 10) strategy, dialogue journals, developing the brain (building off information in other chapters), and intentional teaching. We will then end the chapter with a discussion around developing an anti-bullying environment based on creating an overall safe school environment, also known as a positive school climate.

STRATEGIES

2 × 10 (2 by 10)

The 2 × 10 strategy is based on relationship building. Essentially the strategy states, "Spend 2 minutes per day for 10 days in a row talking with an at-risk student about anything she or he wants to talk about" (Watson, 2015). The reasoning behind the 2 × 10 strategy is to build rapport with all students in the building.

What is the 2 × 10 strategy? Each teacher/staff member is assigned two students. For two weeks the teacher/staff member intentionally spends ten minutes a day with those two students talking about everything and anything except academics. These conversations can include anything from the morning's events to likes and dislikes to television shows or hobbies.

In order to develop strong relationships and a positive and inclusive school classroom, it is highly suggested that all staff members participate in the 2 × 10 strategy. Through these interactions all students feel that someone cares about them and is invested in their lives—relationships are built. As Bronfenbrenner states, "Every child needs to know someone is absolutely crazy about them." Equally important, the entire staff gets to know students at an even deeper level creating opportunities for better communication and keeping track of student concerns and progress. Although it is not clear where this strategy originated, an article distributed by Association for Supervision and Curriculum Development (ASCD) reported that when this strategy was used there was "an 85-percent improvement in that one student's behavior." In addition, he found that the behavior of all the other students in the class improved (Wlodkowski, 1995).

Dialogue Journals

Writing has been proven to be an effective way to both process and communicate feelings and experiences. Teachers from kindergarten through high school have found dialogue journals to be an effective way to learn about their students.

What is a dialogue journal? There is power in writing. Dialogue journals are a place for students write about their lives outside of school. It can include anything from their hobbies, to their families, to their living conditions. The knowledge that educators can gain from and learn about students from these journals is critical to building positive relationships. Furthermore, journals can be used as a safe place to share information that is too difficult to discuss in person. It is important to remember that some information may be difficult to talk about or process. Additionally, students may be fearful that a peer may overhear the conversation.

There are a number of ways in which teachers can ensure journals are a safe space for sharing. In the older grades, teachers can let students know that they are the ones who decide if a journal entry is confidential or not. There are ways to cover up pages so that the teacher does not read that page. Students can be asked to mark pages that they would like to share with the teacher. With younger children teachers can write back, supporting the student in writing, but also learning a great deal of information that young children simply may not be able articulate or developmentally understand fully.

Besides composition notebooks or paper journals, there are many applications teachers and students can use to keep a journal or diary. If the preferred journaling mode involves technology, teachers and students can use one of the many apps available such as Day One, Diarium, Grid Diary or Five Minute Journal. Most apps have a free version, and students may prefer to write on their phones or computers. Whether you are using technology or an old school composition notebook, journals are an effective way to build trusting and supportive relationships with students of any age.

Developing the Brain

We have discussed the brain a great deal in this book, which hopefully indicates the importance of understanding the invisible nature of student behavior. However, in this section we focus on the brain in positive relationships. To start, we are going to ask and answer two questions:

1. Why should educators build relationships with students based on brain science?
2. How can educators help develop the brain through relationships?

The first question of why? It is imperative that students have strong relationships. Through these strong relationships, students are able to more freely move out of the "survival brain" of hypervigilance and into the "learning brain." However, there are also other reasons as outlined by Understood (2020) that focus on brain science, predominately the chemicals released in different situations.

According to Understood (2020), relationships

1. Build motivation.

   Positivity goes a long way. When students experience a positive relationship with anyone, including a teacher, dopamine is released. In the brain dopamine acts like a drug that encourages motivation.

   A frequently used anecdote to describe the effects of dopamine relate to the visual simulations and dopamine releases of social media. "According to an article by Harvard University researcher Trevor Haynes, when you get a social media notification, your brain sends a chemical messenger called dopamine along a reward pathway, which makes you feel good" (McSweeney, 2019). Therefore, the "high" that relates to the addiction levels for social media interactions, is very similar to the impact of positive relationships as it relates to brain science.

   One strategy you can use to develop positive relationships includes the idea that for every one negative interaction, you ensure that you have five positive interactions with that student (1-5+).

2. Create a safe space for learning.

   When students feel safe, they are more likely to let their guard down, laugh, engage in social activities, and bond with peers. This feeling of safety and happiness releases the hormone oxytocin, which is known as the "bonding hormone." This concept relates back to the bottom of Maslow's Hierarchy of Needs, the need for psychological safety. Once students feel safe, a feeling of belonging and bonding (relationships) can begin. When students feel safe they are able to "release the gas pedal" and move from survival mode to learning mode.

   One strategy suggested for creating a safe space through relationships is to accept, embrace, and allow failure in the classroom. Being able to model and cope with failure is a life lesson that creates safety, trust, and a brain ready to learn.

   However, it is important to know the most effective ways to address failure. It has been found that using sentences including "when-then" or asking "I wonders . . ." or even providing a choice for students sends the message to students that there is always more than one right answer.

Explicit conversations with students is also important and can start with watching some of the popular TED Talks focused on the role of failure in success.

Learning is taking risks, and today many companies are more interested in an individual's failure than their success. We know failure breeds success. And we must make sure our students know this is true in the classroom, as well. It is a delicate dance, but in the end creates an environment where students are in their learning brains and not their survival brains.

3. Build new pathways for learning.

   In professional development sessions we tell participants that it is our job to build a "positive rut" in the brains of our students. We want to be so consistent with our relationships and interactions that the rut is so deep that the neurotransmitters have no option but to follow the rut (path). When educators build "positive ruts" with students, we can learn about their interests, experiences, and prior knowledge.

   When educators include students' interests in lessons, connections are made and knowledge is learned. A teacher who understands the important role prior knowledge plays in learning, works to bridge the gap between what students know, and what they want them to learn. Learning that starts with and is connected to student interest and prior knowledge is highly motivating and successful.

4. Improve student behavior.

   Positive relationships have the potential to greatly improve student behavior. Science research tells us that when students see an action modeled or experience a relationship, their brains are activated to mirror the action. This is known as mirror-neuron system. Therefore, modeling is part of relationship building that improves behavior. And as we know, modeling is part of teaching.

   Teachers are modeling positive, or negative behaviors all day, and sometimes without even realizing it. When teachers treat all children with the same amount of understanding, respect and caring, students will learn to emulate that positivity and fairness.

Reflection: What temperament traits are you modeling for students on any given day? How are you, and how are you not, modeling positive, open, respectful and caring behaviors throughout the day? In other words, what signs of caring are you modeling for your students?

Beyond modeling, it is important that we explicitly teach social skills, empathy, turn-taking, and self-regulation, just as you might teach reading or math. In the days of high-stakes testing we have forgotten how important teaching social studies, and social skills are to student overall development. And, as a reminder, when students are living in poverty, the best concept to focus on in social emotional learning (SEL) rather than reading and math (survival brain verses learning brain).

As a result of this test-based education, we are seeing more and more programs pop-up focused on SEL. When a student struggles academically, we give them more instruction in that content. But, all too often if a student does not have the skills to self-regulate, we punish him/her. We need to replace this punitive response with proactively providing instruction in SEL. In chapter 10 you will find numerous literature-based lessons to do exactly that.

In addition, another strategy focuses on morning meetings as outlined by the Responsive Classroom curriculum. The circles or meetings focus on social skills, relationship building, modeling, learning, and many other essential classroom concepts such as building a sense of community, accountability, and can involve fun and engaging learning objectives through games and interactive activities.

Overall, the brain is important in all aspects of interacting and educating all students, especially those living in poverty. Understanding brain development and chemistry is essential when building a safe and inclusive environment.

Reflection: What are some ways that you explicitly teach social emotional development in your classroom? How do you intentionally work toward classroom community building?

Intentional Teaching

What is intentional teaching? While people may have their own definitions based on their experiences and background, the concept essentially means that teachers design classrooms and plan, implement, and assess lessons with a specific goal in mind that is focused and balanced. It is widely accepted that teachers who embrace intentional teaching in their practice use a variety of strategies, many of which we have already discussed. Strategies such as modeling, open-ended questions, shared thinking, and postulating.

Intentional teaching activates the brain in a way that relates to students' backgrounds, realities, and funds of knowledge. It is built on shared interests, discussions, and sometimes spontaneity resulting in learning in the moment. For example, when a group of students experience a similar event, whether it is traumatic or not, the spontaneity of debriefing and discussing is part of intentional teaching. This flexibility and focus on the students builds strong relationships, changes brain chemistry, and creates learners who are ready and eager to learn.

A strategy that goes hand in hand with intentional teaching and educating students living in poverty is the importance of exposure to places outside of the classroom. Leaving the classroom to increase positive exposure can be as simple as a walk through the community, or neighborhood. Members of the community can also be invited into the classroom as a way to expand students' knowledge and exposure, but also to build a bigger sense of community and trust for members of the community.

This idea reminds us of the difference between rural and urban poverty. Students living in poverty in rural areas have different challenges. For instance, it usually isn't possible for teachers in rural schools to simply take students for a walk through the community. Students and families living in rural poverty also don't have access to the same level of public transportation that is present in urban settings, so community resources are spread out and may be far away, and transportation is difficult or sparse. Getting to know the community and being aware of the different challenges between urban and rural poverty are part of intentional teaching.

Of course, field trips are also excellent ways to increase exposure, but if for financial reasons they are not possible, there are many excellent websites for virtual field trips. With virtual field trips, you can take your students through the White House, around the world or universe, and inside a zoo from your classroom, expanding student prior knowledge and potentially leveling the playing field between children in poverty, and their more affluent peers who may have more experiences traveling or visiting museums, and so on.

The intentional or purposeful teaching of relating to reality, but also expanding mindsets and experiences is a foundational piece that can impact the life trajectory of all students, especially those living in poverty.

POSITIVE SCHOOL CLIMATE

Building a school environment that is based on culturally responsive teaching, safety, trust, and respect can be accomplished through many pathways, however one is through the strategy of engaging in anti-bullying planning and implementation, or planning for a positive school climate and culture.

However, before we begin to discuss building a positive school climate that is void of bullying, the term bullying must be defined. Bullying is "a situation where a person, called a bully, verbally or physically threatens or assaults a person, causing the person to feel a real or perceived power imbalance," essentially feeling unsafe (study.com).

Bullying can happen in many formats such as verbal, nonverbal (exclusion), to cyberbullying. While many people generally understand verbal bullying as saying something that is harmful and nonverbal bullying is creating a sense of power imbalance maybe from exclusion, cyberbullying is something that is newer with the current and upcoming generations.

Cyberbullying is defined as "the use of electronic communication to bully a person, typically by sending message of an intimidating or threatening nature." Interestingly, Henion and Holt (2014) found that "cyberbullying isn't just a problem in middle class and affluent areas. Teenagers in poor, high-crime neighborhoods also experience online bullying" (para. 1). While the causes for the cyberbullying may differ by community, the experience and exposure to cyberbullying does not discriminate.

So, what is anti-bullying? Another term often used in bullying prevention, which is the active engagement of all stakeholders to protectively build a community that does not harm, intimidate, or coerce students or groups of people that are seen by others as vulnerable or weak. While there are many groups of people that are bullied and various types of bullying, this section will specifically speak to bullying based on economics and how to build a school community that does not partake in economic bullying. The technical definition of anti-bullying is "laws, policies, organization and movement aimed at stopping or preventing bullying" (study.com).

Students living in poverty often experience bullying because of the food they bring to school, being part of a free and reduced lunch program, not wearing the "right" clothes, not bringing money for school events, and the list goes on. Surprisingly, bullying occurs from both peers and teachers/educators in the building. A teacher who calls out students who have not brought $2 for a field trip, is bullying and economic shaming. Peers who notice and make fun of a student because they wear the same clothes every day, is bullying. It was found that fifteen million students live in extreme poverty in the United

States and arrive on the first day of school without food, new school clothes, and the needed school supplies (Kids in Need Foundation, 2020).

In 2019, USA Today (Ali) reported on a Memphis high school freshman who reported that he was being bullied for wearing the same clothes every day. In this instance, football players at the school came together to gift the student new clothes. While this specific event ended positively, the suicide statistics for students who are bullied are staggering. It has been reported that (The Jason Foundation, 2020):

- Suicide is the second leading cause of death for ages 10–24. (2017 CDC WISQARS).
- Suicide is the second leading cause of death for college-age youth and ages 12–18. (2017 CDC WISQARS)
- More teenagers and young adults die from suicide than from cancer, heart disease, AIDS, birth defects, stroke, pneumonia, influenza, and chronic lung disease, combined.

Due to the crisis of students' experiences of bullying, sometimes resulting in suicide, governments and schools have implemented anti-bullying policies and laws. These are one prevention strategy that can change social norms. While the U.S. Department of Education provided suggested policy principles, researchers have found that three specific components in "anti-bullying laws decreased the odds of a child being bullied by 20 percent. Specifically, these anti-bullying laws had a

- Statement of scope.
- Clear description of the prohibited behavior.
- Requirement that school districts develop, implement, and monitor local policies" (stopbullying.gov, 2017).

To see an example or resource, look to Ohio's and Connecticut's Anti-Bullying Laws and Policies: https://www.stopbullying.gov/resources/laws/ohio

Reflection: What can schools and educators do to create an environment where all students feel supported, welcomed and respected? What conversations have you had as a school regarding explicit teaching of anti-bullying? What specific lessons and teaching strategies do you use in your classroom?

While it is important to know state laws and develop or follow district-wide written policies, it is even more important to actively teach empathy, compassion and anti-bullying lessons. Creating laws and policies is important, but we need to be sure we are not holding students accountable for bullying and prosecuting them according to state law when we are failing to proactively and explicitly teach anti-bullying curriculum in our classrooms and schools. Putting up "zero tolerance zone" posters is not enough.

Although future chapters will provide suggestions/strategies for creating an inclusive and safe environment, one specific strategy many schools implemented within the last five years is something called a Buddy Bench or a Friendship Bench in elementary schools or a lunch app for middle and high schools. A buddy or friendship bench is a designated area on a playground where a student can go if they do not have anyone to play with or want to talk to someone. The school environment, generally peers, are trained to invite that peer to play or to talk to them. "The concept behind the buddy bench, is a simple idea to eliminate loneliness and foster friendship on the playground" (Stevens, 2018).

The concept of the buddy bench entered older grades when a high school student from Sherman Oaks, CA, Natalie Hampton, created an app called "Sit with Us." This app was designed to helps students "who have difficulty finding a place to sit locate a welcoming group in the lunchroom" (Wanshel, 2016) which is arguably one of the most stress-inducing experiences for middle and high school students. "Hampton told Audie Cornish on NPR's 'All Things Considered' that the reason why she felt an app like this was necessary is because it prevents kids from being publicly rejected and being considered social outcasts by their peers."

Both the buddy bench and the app are changes to school culture that can impact the social and learning environment for all students. It was found that students, specifically students who are deemed "cool" by social norms, can reduce student conflict and bullying significantly (Wanshel, 2016) by actively not participating. When we involve the entire school community in combating bullying, it is more effective than punishing the bully, or doing things in isolation in our individual classrooms, especially since much of the bullying occurs on the playground, in the cafeteria, on the bus, and over social media.

When it comes to bullying, role-play is an important strategy for students and teachers alike. One thing that is most difficult for teachers, and all school personnel, is knowing how to respond when they hear shaming and bully-ing happen. We know we must respond immediately otherwise our silence perpetuates the behavior, but in that moment we might freeze and simply not know how to react.

Role-play is a great opportunity for teachers to actually practice how they would respond in these situations. Teachers and all school personnel can act out various types of shaming and bullying in various school settings. What does the bus driver do when she hears a student bully another? How about the cafeteria worker? A teacher walking down the hallway? In order to be confident and competent in these difficult situations, we must practice. This is also an effective tool for family nights.

Parents and caregivers can role-play how to talk with their children or teachers about bullying, how to handle cyberbullying, and so on. The same thing can be said for students. An effective instructional strategy is to have students engage in role-play so they can both develop the skills necessary to handle certain situations, but also develop their empathy and compassion for the victim, as well as their overall understanding of the impact of their behavior.

An example of incorporating many strategies to decrease bullying occurred in elementary first through third grade classrooms. A teacher implemented four lessons, twenty-five minutes each. Over four quick lessons involving various techniques (a read aloud, role-play, labeling the bystander, bully, and ally, etc.) students in grades one through three became well versed in what it meant to bully and be a bystander, and how it felt to be an ally. In fact, we did these lessons right before summer break and in fall a teacher reported that children were discussing bullies, allies, and bystanders on the playground when they returned from summer. These lessons are powerful in that they give children the language needed to be an ally, the confidence to not be a bystander, and the compassion to hesitate before bullying another human being.

CONCLUSION

In addition to these ideas to reflect on and consider, and strategies to building a positive, anti-bullying school environment, there are numerous literature-based lessons in chapter 10. It is not enough to put up zero-tolerance posters and use anti-bullying rhetoric in schools. Nor is it enough, or fair, to develop laws and policies without also actively teaching anti-bullying and anti-shaming pervasively in schools. Perhaps most important, and as stated many times in this book, building relationships with students is critical to both minimizing shaming and bullying, and handling the situation positively and productively when bullying does occur.

Relationships are everything. If we get to know our students, their families, and the students in our school, we can learn about their experiences, and step-in when they are less than positive. If students and families trust us, they will be more likely to be vulnerable and share when they are being mistreated and ask for help. Building positive relationships that are based on active listening without judgment, showing signs of caring, and consistently demonstrating an undivided commitment to a zero-tolerance policy, we can hopefully avoid the worst from happening to our students.

Reflection: We have discussed shaming as it relates to food and money in other chapters. Use that information, and information from this chapter, to reflect on the following:

Food shaming/bullying: Refer back to that chapter/section. Can you think of a time you saw food shaming or bullying in action? How did you handle the situation? Are there any ways in which you or your school unknowingly shame students about food? Are there comments made about the "unhealthy" food brought from home? What is your school lunch policy? Does your school "out" students who receive free or reduced lunch (e.g., stamping their hand)? Do you require students to bring a snack to eat during the day? What do you do if a student doesn't have a snack?

The first thing teachers and school personnel should do is reflect on these questions and immediately modify any practices that contribute to food shaming. It is also important to see food shaming as a form of bullying. At the same time, how does your school actively work to prevent food shaming or bullying related to food? Does your school provide "snack packs" (e.g., weekend blessing bags) for all students, not just students who are low income? Do classroom teachers have snacks in their classroom that all students can access without shame or notice? Do you openly discuss food shaming, food poverty, and food diversity? How? Is there a food bank at or near your school? Are you and all school personnel aware of community support and resources? How do you share that information with families to proactively avoid food shaming (i.e., a family who knows about the food bank may be able to send that student to school with a snack)?

Money shaming/bullying: Refer back to that chapter/section. How does your school participate in money shaming/bullying? Does your school require students to pay for field trips, assignment notebooks, expensive school supplies, or uniforms? If so, how does your school assist all families? Is it up to the low-income family to ask for help? If so, how can you avoid putting families in that position? How do you address clothing shaming? Have you seen students bully other students because of the clothes they wear (i.e., clothes that are dirty or smelly, worn, too small/big or not in style)? What did you do? Are you aware of clothing options within the school? What is the role of your school nurse? How can your school think beyond the notorious big cardboard box of clothing in the nurse's office? Are you aware of secondhand shops and clothing donations in your community? How do you share that information with families?

As one principal in Newark, NJ found out, providing a laundry room with free washing machines and dryers increased student attendance. "My kids weren't coming to school," Principal Akbar Cook stated (Glor, 2019). In this interview with CBS News he continued by saying, "I think we really put the microscope on basic needs of kids. Everyone wants high test scores, everyone wants them to perform well. But if the kid doesn't feel confidence in just coming to school, being that person we know they can be, then what are we doing."

Chapter 8

Supporting Ourselves, and Each Other

You can't pour from an empty cup. You need to take care of yourself first.

Taking care of yourself is being there for your kids, like how on a plane, they tell you to put on your oxygen mask first.

—Gwyneth Paltrow

Burnout, compassion fatigue, secondary trauma. All of these terms are related to caring and nurturing professions, such as education. However, as the quotes above state, it is important for educators to take care of their own well-being so they can be present and prepared for the students that enter their classrooms. Educators, focusing on your mental and physical needs comes before, or in the least coincides, with focusing on the many needs of your students and families. Along these lines, teachers and school personnel need to be able to support each other, just as schools work to support their families.

Reflection: What are some ways that you work together as teachers, school personnel, and administrators to support each other? What are some things that would help you feel like you have a more supportive system in your school?

While burnout, secondary trauma and compassion fatigue are all interrelated, we will begin by discussing them one at a time.

BURNOUT

Teacher burnout is "a state of chronic stress that leads to physical and emotional exhaustion, cynicism, detachment, and feelings of ineffectiveness and lack of accomplishment" (Bourg, 2013). While not every educator experiences burnout, others may experience it at various points in their career. One of the culprits often blamed is the cultural norm in America of overwork or being a workaholic. Remember, you are more than your job.

Although not everyone experiences burnout, there are signs of burnout, which you will notice are very similar to the symptoms of compassion fatigue and secondary or vicarious trauma. Some signs of burnout are shown in table 8.1 (Bourg, 2013; Tapp, n.d.).

So, we know the signs, but what can we do to avoid or decrease burnout? Teaching is unlike any other profession in a number of ways. When students enter the classroom to when they leave for home there is, on most days, little to no time for even a trip to the restroom. When working under these conditions it is difficult to listen to your mental and physical self.

Mary Beth Cunningham, a mental health consultant, once explained to us that we have physical health and brain health. In order to function at our top ability, we need to keep both healthy. This includes taking time for yourself to recharge and being aware of your work-life balance. Remember, you are more than your job.

For teachers, the very way in which that statement may be problematic is exactly why we need to say it. Teachers often do not see their work as a job. Instead, when they think about their day they see their students, their lessons, and their class' concerns or needs. It is easy for teachers who work

Table 8.1 Signs of Burnout

Signs of Burnout
Emotional Signs:
- Anger   - Depression   - Anxiety   - Irritability   - Apathy
- Loss of enjoyment
Physical Signs:
- Loss of appetite   - Weight Gain   - Increased Illness   - Isolation
- Sleep issues (extreme fatigue or insomnia)   - Lack of productivity
Brain Signs:
- Forgetfulness or impaired concentration   - Pessimism   - Detachment

in high-poverty areas or who have concerns for any child in their classroom that is living in poverty to forget about themselves, their lives, and even their family to do everything they can to support all of their students as best as possible. It is during these times especially, that teachers need to have specific self-care strategies.

One strategy that is helpful to use when reflecting on self-care, burnout, and compassion fatigue is to complete a balance wheel. Below is a description of the process. We encourage participants to complete this every six months as a way to check in on one's physical and mental health. One important note for administrators is that teachers need time to self-reflect and engage in self-care. The last thing that teachers, who are struggling to find time during the school year for anything beyond the instruction and students in front of them, need is one more thing to do!

Reflection: Where can you find time during the school day to engage in self-care strategies? How can you team up with another teacher to complete these strategies together? Can you work with other teachers to develop an argument to present to administration for needing this time, with specific logistical ideas?

Balance Wheel Activity

Step 1: Use the wheel provided or draw your own wheel. In each of the open areas write something that is important to you. Examples may include working out, financial stability, family, students, etc.

Step 2: Once each open area is filled, imagine there is a scale in each open area where the zero is at the center and the outside circle is 10. For each identified area rank your happiness/satisfaction/current feeling about each other. When you are done, you will have a dot on the imaginary scale from 1-10 in each open space.

Step 3: Connect the dots. Do you have balance? How do you know? The goal is for the connecting link to be almost a perfect circle. If you have areas that jut up or down, that indicates that you have personal work to do in that one area. Maybe it is taking better care of yourself because you haven't made it to the gym and you are dissatisfied with that. Or maybe you feel as though you are spending too much time working (maybe close to a 9 or a 10), which is impacting the balance in the rest of your life. (figure 8.1)

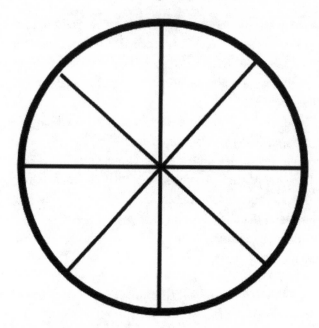

Figure 8.1   Balance Wheel Activity.

SECONDARY TRAUMATIC STRESS

In addition to burnout, teachers also can experience secondary traumatic stress, especially if they experienced trauma as a child, specifically poverty. As a child or an adult, did you experience or are you experiencing living in poverty or low to middle class that is impacting your quality of life? If so, how do you think that is impacting your ability to engage in self-care? Self-reflection is one of the first steps in understanding the impact of secondary trauma in your life (as well as burnout and compassion fatigue).

But what is secondary trauma? It is "indirect exposure to trauma through a firsthand account or narrative of a traumatic event." In the case of this book, we will focus on the traumatic experiences often associated with living in poverty. Each of these questions lead to the root factors associated with secondary trauma: exposure to traumatic events, exposure to someone coping with a traumatic event (e.g., stories from students), and/or helping others while neglecting personal brain and physical health (table 8.2).

Are you experiencing any of these signs? If so, how do you manage them? Or, are you managing them? Telling you to listen to your mental and physical self is easier said than done, we know. But, you can take a moment right now

Table 8.2   Signs of Secondary Traumatic Stress

Signs of Secondary Traumatic Stress		
Feeling numb or detached	Feeling overwhelmed	Low energy (fatigue)
Self-destructive coping	Low job morale	Often confused
Lacking self-satisfaction	Emotionally unavailable	

to check in with yourself. If you notice you are experiencing some of these signs, to whom can you share that with? Identifying secondary traumatic stress and talking about it with someone you trust is the first step to healing.

An additional strategy is to identify your "locus of control" or what you have control over in your life in the lives of your students. Is their home life within your locus of control? Where they sleep, or if they have consistent healthy food? The overall answer is no. Outside of school you have no control of their living situations, safety, or interactions. Bottom line is you can do everything you can to positively support your students and their families during the day, and you can suggest or provide resources, and connect families/students with community support and resources—this is your influence—but your locus of control stops when students exit the school (figure 8.2).

So, what is in your control? Class instruction, relationships, a culture of community, learning and support, behavior management techniques, healthy food during the school day, and anything else within the hours and walls of the school day/building. Also in your control is working with families to best

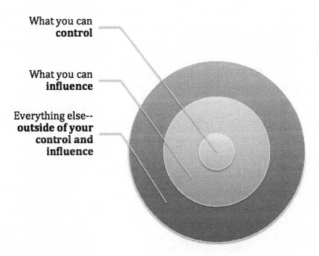

What you can **control**

What you can **influence**

Everything else-- **outside of your control and influence**

Figure 8.2   Locus of Control.

support them at home, and in school. This may include working with members of the community and connecting families with resources/individuals.

A good idea is to web out what you have control of in the lives of your students. Then under each "control" area write the things you do and will do to positively impact the students in that area. You can make a difference through thoughtful planning and interactions. Then, make an action plan for you! How will you learn to separate yourself or engage in self-care? Looking at your web of things that are in your locus of control, work to recognize that you are doing a great deal for your students, and you need to maintain your own balance and health to continue to do so—this is your oxygen mask.

COMPASSION FATIGUE

Compassion fatigue is often used synonymously with the terms "burnout" and "secondary trauma," therefore you will see many similarities. However, "it is slightly different because compassion fatigue is highly treatable and may be less predictable" (GoodTherapy, 2020). The other major difference between burnout and compassion fatigue is that "the onset of compassion fatigue can be sudden, whereas burnout usually emerges overtime" (GoodTherapy, 2020).

The definition of compassion fatigue is an "indifference to charitable appeals on behalf of those who are suffering, experienced as a result of the frequency or number of such appeals" (dictionary.com). Teachers can easily and quickly feel overwhelmed by students' struggles and trauma, especially when there are a number of students experiencing poverty. In table 8.3, the symptoms of compassion fatigue are provided (GoodTherapy, 2020).

Do you recognize the symptoms of compassion fatigue? Can you think of ways you can reenergize yourself and get the support you need? Connections to people, a support system, time in nature, outside of school hobbies,

Table 8.3 Symptoms of Compassion Fatigue

Symptoms of Compassion Fatigue		
Chronic physical exhaustion	Depersonalization	Irritability
Feelings of self-contempt	Difficulty sleeping	Weight loss
Headaches	Poor job satisfaction	Chronic emotional exhaustion

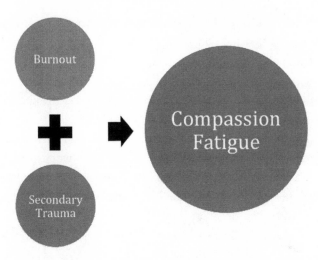

Figure 8.3   Burnout, Secondary Trauma, and Compassion Fatigue. *Source*: Middleton, J. (2015). https://www.aginglifecarejournal.org/addressing-secondary-trauma-and-compas sion-fatigue-in-work-with-older-veterans-an-ethical-imperative/.

and even pets can help alleviate symptoms. It has been found that "being in nature, or even viewing scenes of nature, reduces anger, fear, and stress and increases pleasant feelings. Exposure to nature not only makes you feel better emotionally, it contributes to your physical wellbeing, reducing blood pressure, heart rate, muscle tension, and the production of stress hormone" (University of Minnesota, 2016).

While many times burnout, secondary trauma, and compassion fatigue are used interchangeably or in the same conversation, they all are slightly different. However, a well-known graphic to show the association between the three is in figure 8.3 (Middleton, 2020).

Reflection: Write out the things you worry about the most, the things that keep you up at night. What are they? Are they things you can control? Are they things someone else can control (e.g., school counselor or social worker, town social services, principal, etc.)? Can you have a conversation with your colleagues to gather ideas or just to talk about your concerns?

SUPPORTING EACH OTHER

Throughout this book is the common thread of relationships and the importance of building safe and trusting relationships. Building positive relationships also applies to teachers supporting one another. How do you work together with teachers in your school? The first step to being able to lean on and support each other is building a trusting relationship. When teachers trust each other they can openly and effectively collaborate. When they see themselves as part of a team they can share what is working and ask for support when change is needed.

Once teachers see themselves as part of a team, they will be better able to collaborate on lesson plans, work together to vary instructional strategies, and share ways to effectively communicate with families. When there is trust between teachers they can enter each other's classroom to observe and provide feedback. One program that effectively supports this high level of collaboration is called Teacher Expectation Student Achievement (TESA). As mentioned in other areas of this book, there is a great deal of research that supports how a teacher's expectations of a student can greatly impact that student's performance. TESA states that teachers often do the following:

- Ask more complex questions of higher achieving students than lower achieving students
- Give less wait time to girls and perceived lower achieving students than to perceived higher achieving students
- Call on higher achieving students more often than lower achieving students
- Seemingly provide help to lower achieving students, but in actuality provide help to higher achieving students more often because they seek it
- Spend 25 percent less time listening to lower achieving students than higher achieving students
- Allow lower achieving students to sit in the back of the classroom where they can beignored

When teachers trust each other, they can take turns observing each other, and then share ways they may have approached individual children differently. In this way teachers feel like they are working as a team, supporting each other, and working together to solve problems. Finding time during the school day and after to connect with each other, ask for support, and just talk is important for building positive relationships. Administrators should consider the importance of having time to collaborate and find ways to support teachers in doing so. And, not only to share pedagogical ideas but to support each other mentally and emotionally. No one understands the challenges of teaching better than other teachers.

Some other effective strategies are team-teaching, multiage teaching, and merging classrooms for the entire day, or part of it. When teachers do this they inherently learn from each other, and model positive, close relationships for other teachers in the building. When teachers lead with an open mind, willingness, and interest in working together, everyone benefits.

Reflection: In what ways do you reach out to other teachers to build a trusting relationship? What are some things you could do to show your openness and interest in doing so?

CONCLUSIONS

Teacher burnout, secondary traumatic stress, and compassion fatigue are real. Teachers are so concerned with supporting students and their families that they often forget how to support themselves, and don't have the time or energy to support each other. When we trust ourselves and trust our colleagues, we can work together as a community. In every other field outside of education collaboration is seen as a critical part of growth and success. Yet, teachers are often given few opportunities to work together and, as a result, don't always build the trust necessary to collaborate fully. With a whole school effort, teachers can be given the time necessary to build positive relationships, and support themselves, and each other.

Chapter 9

Supporting Families

Community Resources and More

There is already promising evidence that comprehensive support can promote students' academic achievement and life chances, and it is worthwhile to build on this evidence base.

(Walsh, Sibley, and Gish, 2018)

Parenting or helping raise children is hard, and so much harder if you live in poverty. Like more affluent families, no two families living in poverty have the same needs. Yet, there are things that schools can do to best support low-income families and minimize the strain that many school practices can have on the academic and social well-being of a student and family. As a classroom teacher, the most important thing we can do is work to establish a supportive and positive relationship with family members. As a school, the most important thing we can do is to build relationships through comprehensive services and create a culture of mutual respect.

Reflection: How do you nurture the relationship between your students and their primary caregivers?

If you have raised children or are currently raising children, you can probably pinpoint little things that teachers did that nurtured and supported your relationship with your child/children. Or, maybe you have warm memories of when you were a child and a teacher nurtured your relationship with your family. Little notes that said, "It's clear how much (your child) loves you." Receiving a phone call just to share that your child was talking about you during the day or being sure that your child is in the small group you take when you come in as a classroom/school volunteer. Small gestures like this go far in nurturing the relationship between caregiver and child. Raising children isn't easy. When we, as educators, think about the role we have in supporting the process of building a strong relationship between caregiver and student, it is the little signs and actions as described above that can make a big difference. These actions and words make a difference not only within families but also in the educator's relationship with families.

BUILDING RELATIONSHIPS WITH FAMILIES

The first and most important thing teachers can do to support their students and families is build positive relationships with family members, and as early in the school year as possible. When working with families living in poverty, teachers need to be aware of and let go of any preconceived ideas or assumptions they may have about poverty and enter the relationship open and ready to learn. Believing that some caregivers, specifically caregivers/family members raising students in poverty, have different needs or are not as capable or intelligent as more affluent caregivers is a mistake, and not an effective way to start a trusting relationship.

Every person raising children needs to know that their child's teacher cares: cares about their child as a human being and about their child's academic success. When a teacher leads with care, and approaches caregivers with an eagerness to learn about them and their child, caregivers respond positively. When caregivers know that you respect them, have high expectations that their child will learn and believe he/she has a lot to contribute to the class, they see these as signs of caring.

Nel Noddings, an American philosopher, developed a well-known theory on caring, and believed it to be the foundation of morality. Noddings (2010) believed, "The caring teacher strives first to establish and maintain caring relations, and these relations exhibit an integrity that provides a foundation for everything teacher and student do together" (p. 4). This idea also applies to caregivers and colleagues.

The person or people in a student's life prior to entering a formalized care setting are his/her first teachers, and know the student well. Keeping this in mind, it is necessary that we see our relationship with families as reciprocal.

We have a lot to learn from families and soliciting that information at the beginning of the year sends a clear message that we want to know about their child, and that their opinions and knowledge matter to us.

There are multiple ways to do this. Reaching out to families early in the year, or before the year starts, and having face-to-face or a phone conversation is a positive start. Sending home surveys and questionnaires at the beginning and throughout the year is a great way to solicit information from family members. Teachers could also keep an ongoing journal with family members that goes home weekly and is another opportunity to learn from families about their concerns, experiences, and what they value. There are also numerous apps that teachers can use to communicate with families that provide a quick and easy way to keep your finger on the pulse of where the families, and their child, are throughout the year. The apps increase parent involvement as they provide consistent, fast, two-way forms of communication.

Furthermore, there is the common practice of "home" visits. Before diving into the research behind home visits, some readers may be thinking, "How do you do a home visit for someone who is homeless?" While there are numerous ways to complete home visits, they can also happen at community locations, such as restaurants or libraries. However, encouraging home visits also "normalizes" the child's living arrangement in the sense that you see it, you accept it, and you build a sense of acceptance that will then guide your teaching in the classroom. Basing the concept of home visits in research, it has been found that they are especially important in school districts with low-income and/or immigrant or refugee families who may have a history of negative experiences with schools or are intimidated by the school system in general.

That being said, home visits are completed differently depending on the area, school, or district, however, overall they have been shown to increase attendance and build a strong foundation for positive communication between families and teachers. At these visits it is important to set the expectations for the school year and to complete an interest inventory for the incoming student with the family. An interest inventory can have several questions on it, but generally the teacher wants to get to know the student and family through the inventory. Another idea for a home visit may include providing home kits that include various games and items for students to engage in with family members.

Regardless of the strategy, the information and knowledge we gain from ongoing communication can be used to both better our interactions with our students and direct our instruction. But, it also allows family members to stay abreast with what we are doing in school, and their child's performance. When families are engaged in ongoing communication we build positive relationships with them, resulting in an increased likeliness that they attend school events, volunteer in classrooms, and so on.

Building and maintaining positive relationships with families also creates the most favorable condition for us to work together when problems do arise. If caregivers feel like they can trust us and trust that we care about their child, they are more open to fielding any concerns we have and are less likely to be defensive if we do have to make a negative call. In terms of student behavior and performance, when we have positive relationships with caregivers based on trust and care we are more likely to be able to work together to problematize situations when they arise.

Further, when students know we have ongoing communication and a trusting relationship with their caregivers, they know we are working together on their behalf, and that they are surrounded by adults who care about how they are, and how they are doing in school. When we establish that we see parent (caregiver)-teacher communication as reciprocal, show signs of caring by having high expectations and interests, and treat families and their children with respect, we are well on our way to building positive relationships with all families.

INCLUSIVE SCHOOL PRACTICES

There are numerous things that need to be done on the school level to support families living in poverty.

First, stop asking for money. Every single time a teacher or school asks for money they are setting some families up for embarrassment, shame, and bullying. There are many ways that schools can get around this. Teachers and/or the school itself can find other ways to pay for field trips, school supplies, and so on. Tapping into existing funds or associations such as the PTA/O may be a possibility. Perhaps a better option is to set up a classroom or school-wide anonymous donation system. This way, rather than buy supplies, and so on themselves, families and community members can simply donate money to a fund that covers all student expenses. There are many apps and programs that teachers can use such as Gofundme.com, DonorsChoose.org, AdoptAClassroom.org, ClassWish.org, or Treasures4teachers.org. PTA/O's themselves could set up such a donation and disseminate the funds to classrooms, or a school administrator could setup a donation or fundraising event. Whoever does it, schools and teachers should do everything possible to avoid asking families for money.

Second, increase ongoing professional development for educators on ways to support families living in poverty. As mentioned in earlier chapters, teachers need opportunities to self-reflect and think about what biases or beliefs they may have regarding children and families living in poverty. In addition to this critical starting place, teachers should have the opportunity to work together, collaborate, and share ideas that have had success. This time should also include sharing information on school and community-wide resources, policies, and practices.

Third, find ways to increase school-family communications. Before we discuss the possibilities, it is important to note that we must be aware that not all families feel comfortable entering a school. For some caregivers, school was not a safe or positive environment for them. For others, they may not have succeeded in school so don't feel a sense of belonging. For those caregivers starting with a home visit may help them to feel more connected and comfortable coming in. Schools can offer incentives to caregivers for attending school events such as offering a bag of groceries or bus passes to the first number of family members who come. To do this, schools need to build positive relationships with community members and businesses and tap into potential resources. Perhaps food, restaurant gift cards, grocery store coupons, and so on can be donated that can be used as incentives to bring families into the building.

Further, relationships with bus companies or other public transportation can help with providing transportation to school events (e.g., give a certain number of bus passes, free bus rides on nights of school events, etc.). Of course, urban versus rural poverty are two entirely different experiences and families have different needs. For instance, in rural areas that do not have the same public transportation system as urban areas, schools might be able to organize parent carpools, or work with churches and other community members to provide rides. Schools also have to find creative ways to publicize school events.

If we find out where our families spend much of their time in the community, we can use this important information by being sure to publicize school events in those locations, and other places in the community. Also, important to note, fliers and so on should be multilingual, and not just posted in English.

Fourth, school personnel can work with members of the town to find ways to use the school as a family-community resource center, also known as a school with comprehensive services (i.e., a holistic school). Schools can reach out to churches, businesses, social services, hospitals, and so on to find opportunities to hold their community events in the school. They can also all work together to create a network that supports families living in poverty. An emergency reserve could include food and gas cards, an emergency checkbook, hygiene products, and so on. The school could be used as a community hub by encouraging area businesses and community services to hold their events at the school (e.g., job fairs, adult learning classes, social service events, soup kitchens, thrift store sales or events, etc.).

Schools could tap into school/community volunteers to hold before-/after-school programs, holiday school programs, and events in the summer when many children have lots of free time and experience the "summer slide." Incidentally, there is research that demonstrates that if children were to read only five books over the summer it will prevent them from experiencing the "summer slide." Therefore, it is important to find ways to make sure children don't leave for the summer without books at home and ways to support families in getting to the town library during those months, and so on.

Fifth, support family-community engagement and access to its resources. In addition to bringing the community to the school, there are many ways in which schools can help connect families to the community. Community-wide networks can be developed that provide rides for families to conferences or school events, doctors' appointments, and so on. Schools could also work with community members to hold donation events around the community for coats, shoes, backpacks, food, and so on. The Association for Supervision and Curriculum Development (ASCD) suggests that schools ask parents a series of questions to determine what the obstacles may be to school and community engagement (www.ASCD.org).

As mentioned in an earlier chapter, if we don't ask and listen we can't determine and address the problem. Asking families these questions would allow us to gain that information and discuss potential solutions (Anderson, 2014):

- What are the challenges you face daily? (Our parents have expressed concerns about finding jobs, feeding their families, and even washing laundry.)
- What is the most common complaint you hear from other parents about the community or its schools?
- Are you active in any community events or organizations? If so, what are they and why are you involved?
- Is the school or district a welcoming place?
- What are the top three neighborhood issues that parents face in the district?
- Where do you get information about the neighborhood?
- What businesses do most families in the community frequent?

Sixth, be sure your school goes beyond "zero tolerance" or "anti-bullying" posters. If a school fails to proactively and systematically teach and discuss bullying in classroom instruction and school-wide initiatives, bullying is unlikely to decrease and students' social emotional development suffers.

How do you implement school-wide systematical initiatives? One way is through the use and integration of core curriculum activities, such as read alouds/books (see chapter 11 for literature-based lesson plans), journal writing, or social studies curriculum units. Another is through the practice and implementation of empathy curriculum/education.

Empathy education has been found to reduce the rates of bullying and school suspensions, which could be a result of school violence reduction when empathy is at the forefront of school culture. Additionally, empathy education has been found to increase pro-social behavior, a positive sense of self, graduation rates, citizenship, community engagement, and successful employment (Making Caring Common, 2018). Some of the many empathy education programs and resources are Roots of Empathy, Making Caring Common, The Center for Emotional Intelligence, Start Empathy by Ashoka, The Ripple Kindness Project, and Project Happiness. Additionally, there are many websites with great lesson plans on what it means to be an ally and bystander (Anti-Defamation League (ADL), Human Rights Campaign (HRC), Teaching Tolerance, etc.) and numerous other resources.

Each of these websites, programs, and lesson plans support the important discussion surrounding students living in poverty who desire a safe, respectful, and empathic (trauma-informed) environment. As John C. Maxwell stated in an Educational Research Newsletter (2018), "Empathy strengths your (educator) relationships with students and families and makes you a more effective ally. Hidden biases, misconceptions and unexamined attitudes about poverty can comprise your sense of empathy. People may hear your words, but they feel your attitude" (para 4). As research shows, people (students) who experience trauma have rewired brain that impacts the ability to develop a sense of empathy.

One way schools and communities are helping to build empathy is through person poverty simulations. Through these simulations educators are able to experience the event of making hard decisions in order to help their family survive. However, there are critics who state that to most of the educators this is like "playing a game" and to students actually living in poverty it is not a game (Gains, 2018). Regardless, the empathy muscle needs to be exercised and grown in students and teachers so that safe, inclusive, and welcoming schools are created.

Seventh, make all efforts school-wide. Research supports that schools are much more effective at supporting families living in poverty when efforts are school-wide. As mentioned in earlier chapters, when efforts to support all students, stop bullying, and so on are school-wide, they are more effective as they send a clear message to all students, families, and teachers that this is a community effort, and everyone is onboard.

There are many ways to do this. In terms of addressing the learning gap, schools can create a student buddy system, a mentoring program, and utilize paraprofessionals and other school personnel to immerse students in positive learning experiences. The buddy system is also a good strategy to support parents and families, connecting families with other families, or with teachers or members of the community. Sometimes it is easier for a parent to discuss concerns they have about their child with someone other than the classroom teacher. There are numerous ways a school can utilize the school nurse (i.e., providing clothes, washing, food, naps, etc.).

Schools can also think about the role of the school library, and work with librarians to develop lending a library, hold community events, connect with the town library, and so on.

Schools also must work together to scrutinize their school lunch program protocol and make the changes necessary to eradicate lunch shaming. It is simply not enough to put up "zero tolerance" posters in school hallways. All members of the school community must work together to intentionally teach students how to be allies and work together to eliminate bullying of any kind.

Eighth, schools can work with community members to develop a poverty reduction plan to address factors contributing to family poverty in your community. The fact of the matter is, communities, schools, and teachers can do everything they possibly can to support families living in poverty, and their students are still going to enter kindergarten already behind. As mentioned in chapter 5, research tracks the achievement gap down to eighteen months, where children of more affluent homes have much wider vocabulary and language abilities than children living in poverty. The achievement gap is not due to the fact that schools are failing, they aren't, or that there are more minority students, or that parents today are relying on technology to "parent" their children. The achievement gap exists because we are failing to support all families. It is not an achievement gap, but an opportunity gap. We do not have mandated maternity/paternity leave, we do not have universal preschool, and we do not have adequate food and medical services for all families. Because of this, compared to other wealthy countries, the United States has the second-highest rate of poverty.

Poverty is why we have an opportunity gap, poverty is why we have a pipeline from low reading performance in grade four, to high school dropouts, to prison. We must all work together, stop blaming schools or families, and look beyond our school walls to address this high level of poverty. Working on the community level we might consider neighborhood revitalization initiatives like Head Start or free or reduced preschool, community gardens, summer and after-school programs, community medical support, efforts to eradicate housing discrimination, support food pantries, and more.

CONCLUSIONS

The single most important thing we could do to support families in poverty is build positive relationships. Positive relationships between teachers and families, students and families, students and teachers, families and community members, and teachers and community members. Ensuring that all stakeholders are part of the equation builds a community of people working toward a common goal.

Working together is how we support student academic success. Working together is how we support families. Working together is how we eradicate poverty in our communities. Working together is how we change policies to include and represent the 21 percent of U.S. children living in poverty, and their families. While working together may not always be simple or easy, using the information and steps provided in this chapter, and the chapters before, create a guidance road map for reaching and teaching all students, regardless of their economic status.

Reflection: Make a list of the ways that you actively work to support families. Make a second list of all community resources that you are familiar with in your community. Add some resources that you lack knowledge of or may need to support your students. Now, meet with a team of colleagues and share what each of you are doing and are aware of, compiling everything onto one spreadsheet or chart paper for everyone to see, add to, and bring back with them. In essessence, creating a breathing resource 'binder' as a team.

Chapter 10

Student-centered Intentional Teaching

Signs of Caring

With any student, how we communicate and interact with them may be the most important aspect of successful teaching. We have focused on building positive relationships in earlier chapters, which is the basis for all effective instruction. Showing signs of caring, learning about our students and viewing them as our teachers, having high expectations for achievement, and showing consistent and fair expectations for behavior, are all important aspects of effective teaching. Gary Howard, in his video, *Seven Principles of Culturally Responsive Teaching and Learning (CRT)*, discusses how a culturally responsive teacher is one who consistently shows students how much she/he cares about them (figure 10.1).

When students living in poverty enter classrooms where "relationships precede learning" they may begin to trust that in this space they matter. Hopefully they feel a bigger sense of belonging and see themselves as part of a "learning community." Gary Howard believes that the teacher's cultural competence is directly correlated with student achievement, and that the most important aspect of that competence is demonstrating consistent positive dispositions, or signs of caring. Along these lines, teachers can be sure to establish classroom rules or expectations and consistently model and reinforce those expectations.

Reflection: What are some ways you show your students that you care about them? How do they respond?

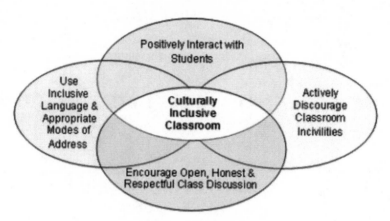

Figure 10.1   Culturally Responsive Teaching and Learning. *Source*: https://teachallreac hall.weebly.com/what-is-culturally-inclusive-teaching.html.

It is also important that teachers take time out to evaluate the classroom climate, and not just in the beginning of the school year. Cornell University's Center for Teaching Innovation proposes the following reasons to focus on creating an inclusive classroom climate:

• Stereotypes may cause alienation and marginalization among those who are the target of unfair generalizations. Students who have experienced stereotypes or expect to be viewed or judged in a certain way may encounter tensions and cognitive disturbances that interfere with learning.
• Instructors can influence the tone of the class environment through their interactions with students and other modes of communication, including the syllabus.
• Student-student interactions both inside and outside of class can affect the overall climate. How the instructor addresses negative interactions will have an impact on student learning.
• Course content that includes a variety of perspectives or that represents multiple views is more conducive to a positive climate.

To do this, students might be given surveys or exit cards and asked specifically to rate the classroom climate, give verbal or written feedback on what is going well, or give suggestions for change. The Center for Teaching Innovation also suggests establishing clear and consistent ground rules and involving students in every step of the process. Some of their suggestions to get started are as follows:

- Decide what is nonnegotiable for you as the instructor.
- Plan to facilitate a conversation around ground rules as a class or present your proposal and give students the opportunity to modify it.
- In small groups, have students think about past learning environments. Which learning environments were productive and positive? What were the characteristics of that environment? Which learning environments were not productive? What were the characteristics of that environment?
- Based on these conversations, have students create a draft list of ground rules for your class.
- Collect and compile these.
- Adjust them as you see necessary and redistribute them to the class for agreement.
- Once everyone agrees, put these ground rules in your syllabus.
- Revisit them throughout the semester to check with students that the ground rules are still working. Make adjustments as necessary.

Reflection: When was the last time you took time to intentionally evaluate your classroom climate? How did you include students in that?

Connecting with your students, working together to create positive learning climates that are inclusive and evolving, setting clear ground rules, using icebreakers, and not shying away from having difficult discussions are all part of creating an environment that supports student learning.

BEST INSTRUCTIONAL PRACTICES

Best practices for teaching children in poverty is in many ways the same as teaching all students, but with even more intention and immersion. For instance, learning about what students are interested in and using that to direct instruction is the beginning of student-centered learning. In addition to ongoing communication, we can survey students and their families, use questionnaires, write journals and more to ascertain their background experiences, interests, and learning styles.

Piaget, as discussed in an earlier chapter, believed all learning is a connection between the known and the new. When we start with students' prior knowledge and connect the learning objectives to what they know, they can better understand the material. Finding out about students' learning styles and intelligences allows us to differentiate our instruction and give choices about how students engage in lessons. Some students may have strong verbal intelligence but not have much success with writing and struggle. In these cases, we can find ways to utilize their strength to support their weakness.

Other students may be kinesthetic learners and need to engage with materials and move their bodies to learn the content of the lesson. When we start with students' background knowledge and interests and differentiate our instruction to accommodate learning styles and intelligences, the learning will be greater. Perhaps most important, when we diversify our instruction like this it is highly motivating and can easily start a positive cycle of student engagement.

Equally important is using consistent data-based assessments to be certain students are being challenged. Teachers must be aware of the downfalls of ability grouping or tracking based on labeling students or having low expectations. Measuring progress frequently, communicating that progress frequently, and involving students (and families) in progress monitoring and goal setting keeps us all accountable for providing challenging learning. Further, when teachers have high expectations for all students, students can begin to recognize that failure is part of, or rather the path to, learning and they will take more risks in the process.

Besides incorporating student learning styles and intelligences, instruction should be fluid or change often, especially when it is clear that it is not working. When instructional strategies vary from working collaboratively to working alone, are student-centered with active meaningful engagement, we are setting the stage for more productive and positive learning. Yet, we also need to consider how we assess learning and apply the same ideas.

In order for any assessment to have validity, it must assess what we actually want it to assess. For instance, if I am assessing whether or not a student understands a math concept by using a worksheet that the student cannot read, I am not assessing what I set out to. This example is especially important since students living in poverty may not be reading on grade level but can certainly understand concepts that are often assessed via reading (e.g., science, social studies, etc.). Varying and differentiating how we assess students allows us to get a more accurate depiction of what they understand.

Overall, being flexible and giving students choices of instructional strategies and assessments would allow us to deepen learning, better evaluate what students understand, and identify what they don't so we can review the material.

Bandura's theory of perceived self-efficacy is an important concept when working with all students, especially students living in poverty since they often come to school without the same experiences and background knowledge as their more affluent peers. Bandura defined self-efficacy as "people's beliefs about their capabilities to produce effects." He believed that when students were self-efficacious toward the presented learning, they were more motivated and more persistent in their attempt to understand the material.

There have been a plethora of studies since Bandura's that validate the critical role of confidence in learning. When a student perceives that he/she can accomplish a task, they will engage, and work harder. Students living in poverty may not have experienced a high level of academic success in the past and bring a lack of confidence into new learning. Bandura believed there are four main ways to increase a student's perceived self-efficacy.

He believed students develop increased self-efficacy by having "mastery experiences" (success increases our belief that we can succeed), by having "vicarious experiences through social models" (witnessing others like us succeed increases our beliefs about our own abilities), by "social persuasion" (when others model high beliefs and expectations that we can learn we begin to believe it, too), and by "reducing people's stress reactions and alter their negative emotional proclivities and misinterpretations of their physical states" (being aware of the role our emotional state plays in our ability to succeed protects our confidence—not doing well on a test because we are nervous, not understanding class content well because we are not in a learning-positive mood, exhausted, hungry, worried, etc.).

Essentially, if we take a student-centered approach to teaching, we can best support students in developing academic success; this success builds confidence, which in turn results in more success, and a positive cycle toward building a more efficacious, engaged, and successful learner has begun.

Reflection: How can you make sure all students have successful learning or "mastery" experiences? How about "vicarious experiences through social models"? What are the ways you use "social persuasion" or show all students that you have high expectations for them? Do you have open discussions with students about how it is understandable that their physical and emotional states impact their ability to learn? Discuss solutions.

CONCLUSIONS

Student-centered intentional teaching starts with showing consistent signs of caring. When educators show they care, they get to know their students. As a result, the classroom interpersonal environment is positive, inclusive, and conducive to learning. When intentional educators get to know their students, they are able to differentiate their instruction and start with what students know, creating a bridge between student prior knowledge and curriculum. Intentional educators also realize that many students may not have the same amount of rich experiences and background knowledge as others, and they work to fill the gaps and create a more level playing field for learning. In these classrooms, all students can experience success, and that success breeds more success. All students can learn, and when educators truly believe that, they are off to a great start.

Chapter 11

Literature-based Lesson Plans

Supporting Students in Poverty

In the research on children living in poverty, it has been revealed that ongoing violence and negative living conditions can decrease children's sense of empathy (Gleason, Jensen-Campbell, & Ickes, 2009). Over time, children may become desensitized and disempowered. Other researchers have studied the relationship between low empathy and bullying (Jolliffe & Farrington, 2006), and empathy as a predictor of one's willingness to defend the bullied (Nickerson, Mele, & Princiotta, 2008). It has been well established that ongoing exposure to violence and intolerance can negatively impact children's understanding of, and desire for, social justice. Children's books have been used as a therapeutic and effective way for teachers to start discussions with their students about controversial or difficult topics (Rozalski, Stewart, & Miller, 2010).

To foster empathy and develop deep understandings of social justice, children who participate in book-centered discussions and role-playing activities learn the concepts of empathy, the power of actions, and develop a strong sense of self. With the recent increase in intolerance and bullying in schools, and on a national level, this kind of empathy education is timely and imperative.

When implementing multicultural or social justice lessons designed to explicitly open up critical discourse, it is important to be sure of a few things. First, it is important for educators to reflect on the topic, their views, potential biases, experiences, and so on. As discussed, all multicultural or social justice education should start with teacher self-reflection. One aspect of this reflection is examining the classroom environment to determine whether or not it is a safe space for all students.

As Lisa Delpit reminds us in *Other People's Children*, when we open up discussions on hard topics with which our students may have experience, a lot of difficult feelings can emerge. The classroom must be safe for this to happen, and safe when it happens. Teacher self-reflection is important to prepare for feelings that may emerge and to proactively develop ground rules for discussion.

Second, it is important that, regardless of age, we allow enough time to talk and process the topics that come up. Without doing so, it is difficult to know what students understand and how they are feeling. This can also be done through writing where, after allowing for oral responses to text, students can write in reading response journals or write letters to characters.

Third, the focus of any social justice education should be on empowering, not disempowering, students. Discussions of injustice and discrimination evoke lots of feelings and it is easy for students, and adults, to feel disempowered. This disempowerment can easily turn into shutting down or developing a sense of apathy. When educators and students discuss these feelings together they can work collectively to find ways to advocate for justice and as a result discover how the little things we do can have big impacts.

Fourth, and along those lines, it is important to be sure to have the perspective that social justice education is not just about empathy building and feeling sorry for individuals or groups, or even raising money/service. Louise Derman-Sparks in Addressing Inequity with Antibias Education: Learning about Economic Class and Fairness reminds us how we must be sure that our focus is on how poverty is a great injustice that happens within sociopolitical contexts, not on charity.

She warns us to avoid activities that come off as helping "poor people," which can unintentionally convey messages of the superiority of the helper and the helplessness of the receiver, and suggests educators frame activities as "making things fair" rather than "helping the poor," says Derman-Sparks and Edwards (2020). Educators should be certain to keep the focus on helping their students understand where poverty comes from and what needs to happen to address the issue. From this, students will come to understand that individuals living in poverty are not very different from them, are not to blame, and do not just want our empathy or sympathy, but our awareness and advocacy.

Fifth, using literature is a great way to bring in any issue related to diversity and social justice. Reading children's or young adult books with students is effective because it depersonalizes issues, therefore making it easier for students to engage—they see it as not about them or people close to them but about the characters in the text. Using books in this way has been referred to as bibliotherapy for a good reason.

Lastly, educators should also be careful when reading books about poverty that their students living in poverty do not feel that everyone is talking about them, feeling sorry for them, or singling them out. Building positive relationships, creating safe environments, and having difficult and honest discussions will help with this, along with the fact that, hopefully, books on poverty are just one of the multicultural/social justice topics your class reads about and discusses all year.

Reflection: How do you use books to engage in social justice discussions or bring diversity into the classroom curriculum and discourse? List some of your favorite books that address issues related to children and families living in poverty, and share with a team of colleagues.

PRESCHOOL-KINDERGARTEN

Teacher reflection: Preschool and kindergarten teachers are in the ideal position to help all students develop positive self-image, self-worth, and confidence. It is also a good time to help students understand that what we wear or have does not define who we are. Children at this age understand social justice, they are keenly aware of when things are, or are not, fair and we can support their sense of empathy and compassion by explicitly discussing what it feels like to be told you can't play because of what you are wearing, and so on. Having these discussions often with children's books, puppets, and role play helps children to develop confidence in themselves and understand what it feels like to be teased. Social studies curriculum in PreK-K often focuses on developing a strong sense of self as an individual, and one's family. Also important at this age is to help students develop social emotional skills.

PreK-K Lesson Plan #1

Focus: Sense of self, self-worth, belonging, individuality, acceptance.

Book Title: *I Like Myself!* by Karen Beaumont and illustrated by David Catrow and *I am Enough* by Grace Byers.

Key Vocabulary: Self-acceptance, confidence.

Before reading: Gather around on the rug and ask the children what they like about themselves. List some of those things on large easel paper. Ask them if they ever felt sad about themselves or didn't like themselves. Discuss why and what made them feel better. Show the cover and ask for predictions. *How do you think she is feeling? Do you think she likes herself? How do you know? What are some things you think she likes about herself?*

During reading: Allow children to discuss the story as you read. Find a good place to stop briefly and ask, "So now do you think she likes herself? How do you know?"

Post reading: Immediately when done reading the book allow children to freely discuss. What kinds of connections are they making? Then look to the list of things they liked before reading and ask them if there is anything they would like to add to the list. *Can we come up with more things that we like about ourselves? Can you tell me some things you like about a friend?* Then read the list. *So, friends, when we don't feel so good about ourselves we should remember all of these things, the things we like about ourselves. Sometimes people don't like themselves because of things like the clothes they wear or how small their house is or how old their toys are. But those things aren't about you, they are just things. Right?* Discuss.

Extensions: Get students in a circle and tell them you have the most important thing in the whole world in the box you are holding. Tell them you can share with them but they have to promise to not tell the secret until everyone has held the box. Start with the first student and have them open the box. The box is empty but glued to the inside of the cover is a mirror. Students may be confused at first but when they see themselves in the mirror they realize that they are the most important thing.

PreK-K Lesson Plan #2

Focus: Awareness of food poverty, empathy building, advocacy, charity, service.

Suggestion: Please do NOT use food for arts and crafts and instructional materials!

Book Title: *The Very Hungry Caterpillar* by Eric Carle.

Key Vocabulary: Hunger, poverty, soup kitchen, food bank.

Before reading: Before reading ask how many children know the book. Tell them that today you are going to focus on something slightly different, but really important. Ask them if they ever remember a time when they were really hungry. What did that feel like? Did you get something to eat? What if you didn't? Let them know that there are many children who don't have enough food to eat. That there are people with empty refrigerators and kitchen cabinets and people who don't have homes and need to go to other places to eat like food banks and soup kitchens. Ask what they would do to help someone who didn't have enough food.

During reading: Discuss how hungry the caterpillar is, and how he eats and eats and that makes him strong and healthy. Stress the importance of food, how we need food to grow and stay healthy and to learn—that it is really hard to learn in school when we are hungry.

Post reading: Allow children to freely discuss the story. Help them to make connections to what they said pre-reading. Engage in shared writing by making a list of things children say they would or could do to help someone who is hungry. Help them think of things like not throwing food out, sharing our snacks with others, not using food for art, donating food to the banks/soup kitchens, and so on.

Extensions: Send a letter home to families letting them know that you discussed food poverty today and that students were working together to raise awareness, and so on. See how you can help the students take their ideas into action. Collect information from the local soup kitchen and food banks to send home so families with need have the information and other families can donate. Write a letter together to the school kitchen or cafeteria asking what they do with leftover food.

PreK-K Lesson Plan #3

Focus: Wemberly worries about everything. The focus here is on social emotional development and stress or worry.

Book Title: *Wemberly Worried* by Kevin Henkes.

Key Vocabulary: Worry, stress, fear, meditation, breathe.

Before reading: Before reading ask students if they ever felt worried about anything. Ask, do you know what that word means, to worry? Allow them to discuss the things they worry about and then make a list on large chart paper. Ask for book predictions. What do you think Wemberly is worried about?

During reading: Find places to make connections between Wemberly's worries and the student's.

Post reading: Allow for student-centered discussion. Then ask them what things Wemberly worried about. Connect back to the things they worry about. Then ask, what can we do when we are worried? Take student suggestions and write a list of things students can do when they are worried on large chart paper to be placed on a wall for future reference.

Extensions: Take a photo of the list of things we can do when worried or scared that you created with students and send a copy home to families. Ask students to lay down on the floor and place a small stuffed animal on their stomach. What happens to your animal friend when you take deep breaths? Let us make our friend go far down, and far up three times.

PreK-K Lesson Plan #4

Focus: Needs and wants, priorities, in-style, peer pressure, and what is most important—family.

Book Title: *Those Shoes* by Maribeth Boelts.

Key Vocabulary: Thrift shop, secondhand store, afford.

Before reading: Ask the students if there is something they want that they can't have. Have they ever been told they can't have something? How come? What was the reason they couldn't have it? How did they feel? Ask, what do you think the boy in this book wants? How do you know? Do you think he can have it? Why not? What do you think he does?

During reading: Stop to ask predictions and briefly discuss key vocabulary like thrift shops. Ask if anyone has ever been to one. Connect to the predictions made before reading.

Post reading: Allow for student-centered discussion first. Then connect to pre-reading discussion and predictions. Did he get the shoes? What did he do? What did he learn? Summarize how, after finding the shoes he wanted in a thrift store but a size too small and wearing them anyway causing lots of pain, he discovered what was most important was his family, especially gramma. Also, emphasize how who he is and who he loves is more important than the clothes he wears.

Extensions: Have children dress dolls with a variety of clothing, discussing how what we are is not who we are, and wearing used clothes or hand-me-downs is totally okay. Or, set up a dramatic play center on dress up or thrift shop and have similar discussions.

PreK-K Lesson Plan #5

Focus: Community, poverty, single parent home, saving money, overcoming obstacles, love over material loss.

Book Title: *A Chair for My Mother* by Vera B. Williams.

Key Vocabulary: Determination, saving (money), loss, hardworking, material items.

Before reading: Ask, why do you think it is called A Chair for my Mother? Why does her mother need a chair? Why do you think she wants to get her one? What does the cover look like? Why do you think it is a restaurant? Prepare students for the loss of the chair (though fire) by asking if they ever had something they loved ruined or lost.

During reading: Be sure to allow for discussion around the characters loss of material things through fire.

Post reading: Allow for free discussion first. How did they get the chair? They saved money in a jar and the community pitched in. Why did mom need a chair? She worked long days on her feet as a waitress? They lost everything in the fire, but then what happened? So they realized that family and friends are more important than material things. Has anyone ever had a fire? Allow for feelings.

Extensions: Make a list together on chart paper of all the things children can do to help their family members who work multiple jobs. What can they do around the house to help out? Are their neighbors who could also use help? What could you do for them?

GRADES 1–3

Teacher reflection: Clearly self-worth, acceptance, and confidence is still a focus in first through third grade, but children at this age are able to better understand and have more life experience with social injustice, and the power of bullying. They are able to understand what it means to be a bully, an ally and a bystander and they know what it feels like to be discriminated against—if even on the playground. They are also better able to organize and collaborate to work together toward change. Children at this age can engage in more reading and writing so supporting them in writing letters to politicians and local community members is a great way to support processing their feelings and developing a sense of empowerment and advocacy. Social studies curricula in grades 1–3 often includes units on needs and wants, the role of community, and social justice issues like poverty and racism, all of which integrate easily into book discussions on poverty.

G1–3 Lesson Plan #1

Focus: *Friendship, gratitude, family, love, social action.*

Book Summary: When you live in a poor urban neighborhood surrounded by homeless people, dirty and unsafe sidewalks and more, it may seem there is little that is beautiful. Although the girl on the cover looks happy, the book takes a decisive and difficult turn on the first page, showing what it looks like to live surrounded by poverty. Yet, the girl's journey through her community reveals she is surrounded by beauty—beautiful people, who empower her to change what she can. While the images are powerful and provoke sadness, you can focus on how she has a network of people in her community who care about her, and she learns that they are what is beautiful, and most important.

Book Title: *Something Beautiful* by Sharon Dennis Wyeth. Illustrated by Chris Soentpiet.

Key Vocabulary: Homeless, dark alley, shelter, courtyard, poverty, change agents.

Before reading: Gather around the rug and ask children what they think "beautiful" means. Ask, what do you think is beautiful? What is most beautiful to you? Write a list of the things/people/and so on. that they say is beautiful. Hold up the book and ask for predictions. What do you notice about this girl? Is she happy? How can you tell? Why do you think she is happy? The title is *Something Beautiful*. What do you think is her something beautiful?

During reading: After the fourth page when the character asks, "Where is my something beautiful?", stop and allow the children to respond. Let the concerns/feelings/thoughts flow. The book started in a much different way than they expected based on the cover. Allow them to discuss the homeless woman, the word "die" on the door, how the young girl must be feeling, and so on before moving on. Then continue and read the rest of the story allowing for quick pauses after each page, and some student to student comments (without inviting the comments to be shared whole group).

Post reading: After reading allow for free response. Notice what connections they are making and concerns. Emphasize how even though she lives in a poor area she has plenty of beautiful things. Emphasize what she did at the end, how she cleaned up and changed things herself. Ask the children what her beautiful "things" are. Make a list, for example, her mom, her friends, playing and dancing, a neighborhood full of people she knows, the apple, her Aunt Carolyn, the baby, and so on. Compare the things she has to the list you made of the things your students said were beautiful to them before reading the book. Ask if anyone would like to add or change what they think is beautiful. Ask how they feel when they have those things/people/and so on. Discuss poverty and how she didn't have many things, but she had people, and love, and that was all she needed to have the strength to change the things she didn't like. Ask, is there anything in your life you'd like to change? How can we work together to help with those things you'd like to change?

Extensions: This book is an excellent introduction to the Needs and Wants social studies curriculum unit. Have students go home and ask their family members what is something beautiful in their life. Then have students write about their something beautiful and make a class big book of Our Something Beautiful.

G1–3 Lesson Plan #2

Focus: Hunger, food poverty, food bank, friendship, collaboration.

Book Titles: *Maddi's Fridge* by Lois Brandt.

Key Vocabulary: Food impoverished, nutritious, secret, embarrassment, worry, empathy.

Before reading: Before reading ask students if they know what it feels like to be hungry. Ask what they do when they're hungry and what if they didn't have food during those times. Ask if they know what a secret is, and if they have ever had a secret. Ask about the title and what they think that means. Make more predictions about the story.

During reading: Allow for short discussion when you discover Maddi's fridge is empty.

Post reading: Allow for free discussion. Then ask the students about the secret, what was it? How did Maddi's friend handle that secret? Is there a time when it is important to not keep a secret? When and why? Share with the students how sometimes we don't know if people we know have food or not. Discuss how Maddi didn't complain and without seeing her freidge her friend would not have known. Discuss why. Was she embarrassed? Come up with ideas together on what we could all do to help people who don't have food when they're hungry, or who have an empty fridge. Discuss food banks, soup kitchens, and so on. Discuss nutritious food and food waste.

Extensions: Make lists of good and bad food choices, but discuss how when you have little choice about what to eat, you eat what you have and that's okay. Openly discuss how sometimes people are teased because of the food they have or don't have. Ask if they have ever seen that happen. Role play or act out what they could do if they see someone being food shamed, or someone hungry, and so on. Take this as an opportunity to discuss how no one has to ask for a snack if they don't have one, everyone is welcome to take some of the classroom snack without asking.

G1–3 Lesson Plan #3

Focus: Community, neighbors, working together, food poverty.

Book Title: *Stone Soup* by Jon Muth.

Key Vocabulary: Trickster tale, contributions, community, townspeople.

Before reading: Ask students for predictions. What do they think about the title? Can you make a soup from stones? Ask what kind of soups they have eaten and what is in them. Notice how the characters are looking into the pot and smiling, predict why.

During reading: Stop in places where the author infers that the monks are tricking the townspeople. Allow for discussion as it becomes clear that if everyone contributes something we can make a nutritious soup together.

Post reading: Allow for free discussion. Ask students what happened in the story—why did the monks trick the townspeople to make a community soup (to get the community to work together and act as a community) and did the people realize they had been tricked, and so on. Ask the students if they think the townspeople will continue to support each other and work together. Ask for ideas on how we could all work together as a community to support each other. List these ideas on chart paper. Follow through.

Extensions: Ask for leftover food from the cafeteria or kitchen and make a class soup together. Or, make a friendship salad, or something that everyone can contribute to (picking from food choices already in the classroom) to show how when we all work together we can make community food to enjoy together. Discuss community gardening. Is there a community garden in your community? Is there space at your school to start a small garden? What could you grow in pots (tomatoes, etc.)?

G1–3 Lesson Plan #4

Focus: Selling home to move into an apartment, moving, poverty, material items/possessions

Book Title: *Yard Sale* by Eve Bunting.

Key Vocabulary: Eviction, yard sale, moving, downsizing, poverty, possessions, material items, afford.

Before reading: Ask the students if they have ever had to move before, not because they wanted to, but because they had to. Ask what that felt like. If they haven't, ask if they ever moved before. Was the change difficult? Tell the students this family has to sell their house because they can't afford to live there anymore. They also have to have a yard sale to sell their possessions to make money. How do you think that feels? Do you think it is hard to sell your things? Discuss how sometimes people have tag sales or yard sales because they just want to sell things they no longer need, other times they need to sell things for money for living expenses. Ask for more predictions on the story.

During reading: Stop and allow for discussion in sad parts of the story.

Post reading: Allow for free discussion. Ask students how the main character felt in the end. Scaffold a discussion around what is most important, family and love over bigger houses and material items. Discuss why some people need money (job loss, health problems, etc.) and must sell their house. Ask for suggestions on how we might work together to help. Write letters to politicians and community members to share concerns around poverty.

Extensions: Ask students if they have anything they would be willing to sell in a school yard sale to raise money for families or trade with another student in the classroom as a way to bring "new/gently used" things into our lives. Incorporate math curriculum units on money, bartering, trade, and so on. Discuss ways we can be there for someone who had to move or was homeless. What are some things we could do that does not involve money? How can we support each other?

G1–3 Lesson Plan #5

Focus: Bullying, allies, bystander, clothing shaming.

Book Title: *I Walk With Vanessa* by Kerascout.

Key Vocabulary: Bullying, allies, bystander, clothing shaming.

Before reading: Discuss if they have ever been teased before or bullied. Has anyone said they wouldn't play with you because of how you look (your clothes, skin, etc.)? How did that make you feel? What would have made you feel better? How did you handle the situation? Introduce "bystander" and "ally." Would you be an ally or a bystander if someone wouldn't play with someone else because of how they looked? Predict the story. Who do you think Vanessa is? Why is it called I Walk With Vanessa? Do you think that person is her friend? How do you know? Do you think she is a bystander or ally?

During reading: Be sure to allow for discussion in difficult moments and predictions.

Post reading: Allow for free discussion. Ask students if she was Vanessa's friend and an ally, both or just one? Why did no one else want to walk with or play with Vanessa?

Extensions: Engage in role play with students. Hand out four role cards: victim, bully, bystander and ally. Ask students to act out their given scenarios. How did it feel to be a bystander and just watch without saying anything? An ally? Bully?

GRADES 4–5

Teacher reflection: While all the things stressed in previous grades are still important, students in grades 4–5 are ready for more complex material. They have more of an ability to identify and communicate feelings and concerns, and are often independently reading books on somewhat intense topics already, making it even more important to read books together with student-centered discussions. Students in grades 4–5 have more life experience to connect and use in problem-solving, as well as in working together to confront issues of poverty and discrimination. Books on poverty are easily integrated into social studies curricula on issues of democracy, government, civil rights, classism, politics, American history, and so on.

G4–5 Lesson Plan #1

Focus: Different perspectives, poverty, socioeconomic status, classism, discrimination, segregation.

Teacher reflection: A father and daughter enter a park at the same time a mother and son enter, but from very different perspectives. It is clear that father/daughter live in poverty, as reflected in their park entrance, which is completely different from the park entrance the mother and son used. There are so many stereotypes to discuss, in both the text and illustrations. While the mother exhibits classist beliefs and is angry at her son for playing with a child of poverty, the children immediately take to each other and fail to even notice their differences. Read this book carefully before sharing with students and think about all the stereotypes presented and how you would discuss them.

Book Title: *Voice in the Park* by Anthony Browne.

Key Vocabulary: Low-income, less-affluent, classism, discrimination, segregation.

Before reading: Ask the students if they have ever gone to a city park. Discussion is dependent on if students live in urban, suburban or rural communities. Ask if anyone has ever been to Central Park in New York or a big city park before. Ask if they have ever played in a public place and had someone not want to play with them. Ask questions that scaffold whether or not they have ever felt judged or discriminated against. *Has anyone ever not played with you because of your clothes or your skin or . . .? How did that make you feel?* Hold up the book and ask for predictions.

Doing a picture walk before reading is important with this book since there are four characters with their own section and font. Consider asking for four volunteers, one to read each part. You could also do this on the second reading. It is definitely a good idea to read this book more than once.

During reading: Allow for discussion and for pauses when each character takes over. Scaffold what is happening in the story, that the book is about four characters who are sharing their experiences and perspectives about the same moment in time.

Post reading: Allow for free discussion. Ask students what was happening, how are the characters related to each other, who is with whom (the girl is with her dad and the boy is with his mom). Ask how they describe the characters—are they happy? Who is happy and who is not? Discuss how the unhappy mom and son came from a very rich looking section of the park and the happier dad and daughter came from a low-income side. Discuss all the evidence that dad and daughter are poor or do not have much money (dad looking for job, etc.) and the evidence that mom and son were rich. Discuss how mom did not want her son to play with the girl. Discuss why. Discuss segregation. Discuss terms like less affluent, low income, and classist. Compare this to the pre-reading discussion on a time when you were judged by your clothing, and so on.

Extensions: The illustrations of this book are loaded with stereotypes, that is, the homeless person on the sidewalk holding a sign that says, "Many children, need food." Put the word "stereotype" or "prejudice" in the circle of a web graphic organizer. Ask students what the word means and list the things they say on the web. Ask for examples of times they experienced prejudice or stereotyping. Hand out paper plates. Have students draw a picture of themselves with multicultural crayons and markers on the outside of the plate. Then next to their picture put a few words that describe the things people have or may assume about them. Then on the inside of the paper plate have students write the truth about themselves or the things they would want people to know about them. For example, on the outside someone might write "short or weak" or "not smart" on the inside write, "strong" or "good at reading." Share.

G4–5 Lesson Plan #2

Focus: Peer pressure, individual preference, shame, bullying.

Book Title: *A Bad Case of Stripes* by David Shannon

Key Vocabulary: Peer pressure, bullying, ally, bystander, shame, fitting in, embarrassment.

Before reading: Ask students if they know what peer pressure is? Ask if they have ever felt they couldn't share something about themselves because they worried they would be teased or embarrassed. Ask if they have ever heard someone shame someone else, make fun of them or pressure them to do, wear or say something. How did they handle the situation? Predict the story.

During reading: Allow for discussion and predictions

Post reading: Allow for free discussion. Ask students why she had a bad case of stripes and what the cure was. How do they think it worked out when she decided to go ahead and eat lima beans? Discuss ways to handle peer pressure.

Extensions: Make a list with students of things they have done or could do when they experience peer pressure. Role play. Discuss why they think someone would pressure someone, what is that about? On large construction paper ask students to make a large stick figure and write down all the reasons why someone would pressure them—who is that person? Then turn it over and make a second person and write all the things they could say or do when experiencing peer pressure (enlist a friend, tell someone, etc.).

G4–5 Lesson Plan #3

Focus: Statistics on poverty in America such as food poverty, electricity, school, and so on.

Book Title: *If America Were a Village*, by David Smith.

Key Vocabulary: Food poverty, water poverty, national statistics, village.

Before reading: Ask predictions for how many people in America have enough food to eat, or how many have electricity or homes, and so on. How many people do they believe live in poverty?

During reading: As a nonfiction book it's good to read the introduction and then ask students which topic on the table of contents would they like to hear first. Make predictions for that area, then read and discuss. Do the statistics surprise students?

Post reading: Discuss ways you can work together to lower the statistics. Discuss why they think people live in poverty. Expose any negative thoughts about people living in poverty and discuss how poverty happens. Discuss ways to work together to prevent poverty in America.

Extensions: Have students chose a topic in the book, food poverty, electricity, ethnicity, and so on, and do their own research on their town, community, and/or state. Have students come up with questions they want to know and then help them to find credible websites by providing a list. Students can scan for that information and report back to the class.

G4–5 Lesson Plan #4

Focus: Poverty, community, homelessness, empathy.

Book Title: *The Can Man* by Laura Williams.

Key Vocabulary: Homelessness, urban poverty, perspective.

Before reading: Ask the students for predictions. What does the can man mean? Why does he collect cans? What do you think he does with the money he makes? What are some ways that students or their families have collected money? Ask what they think the boy is doing, who he is, and what they notice about him.

During reading: Find places ahead of time to stop for predictions like when the boy, who is gathering cans to buy the skateboard he wants but his family can't afford, is close to having enough money and keeps bumping into the can man. What is he going to do? Does he feel bad that he is taking cans/money from the can man? Why? What might he do?

Post reading: Allow for free discussion. Were they right in their predictions? What would they do if they were him? Would they buy the skateboard? What if they needed the money for another purpose like food for their family, would that be different?

Extensions: Ask students to write what purposes they think would validate not giving the collected cans over to the can man. Start a class or school can drive. Car wash? What other ways could they work together to raise money to help each other?

G4–5 Lesson Plan #5

Focus: Poverty, clothes shaming, bullying, bystander and ally, immigration.
  Book Title: *The Hundred Dresses* by Eleanor Estes
  Key Vocabulary: Shaming, bullying, ally and bystander, immigration.
  Before reading: Ask students if they have ever been judged or teased because of the clothing they were wearing. How did they handle the situation? How did it make them feel? Predict the story. What would The Hundred Dresses have to do with clothing shaming? Discuss how this book was written in 1945 but that it is still popular.

During reading: Discuss where she was from, Poland, and what immigration means. Find perfect places to stop and predict. Be sure to stop to "feel" during all the times where she is teased mercilessly. Allow for responses to that.

Post reading: Allow for free discussion. Discuss terms like clothing shaming and prejudice. Discuss clothing, why it is not who we are, but why there is pressure to wear certain things. Where does that come from? Discuss how Maddie, who was a bystander during the teasing her friend Peggy received for having to wear the same dress to school every day, was upset with herself and swore she would never be a bystander again. Role play bystander and ally. How does it feel?

Extensions: Research clothing. Why is there so much pressure to wear "popular" clothing? What makes it popular? What is the role of the media? Who is making money off of trends? Discuss trends and how they come and go. Allow students to do research on clothing trends by picking a trend or piece of clothing or shoe or name brand and research it.

GRADES 6–8

Teacher reflection: While all the things stressed in previous grades are still important, students in grades 6–8 are ready for more complex material that can be used as a reflection piece. They are also ready for stories that might influence their own social action piece, such as doing something to decrease inequity. Students in grades 6–8 are not only trying to learn, but they are also into the stage of life focused on peer influences and being "accepted." Therefore, the teacher will need to have structured, yet open ended interactions in the classroom focused on the reading material. Book on poverty are easily used as an interdisciplinary concept.

G6–8 Lesson Plan #1

Focus: Social class, Economic class, bullying, coping strategies.

Book Title: *Invisible Lines* by Mary Amato, illustrated by Antonio Caparo.

Before reading: Discuss inequities based on money. Discuss how people may treat each other if someone is rich and another student is poor. How do you think that makes the people involved feel? Also discuss challenging that students may be facing and brainstorm ways they work to overcome those challenges.

During reading: After each chapter have students complete a written or verbal (recorded) reflection. Another suggestion that author makes is to put the key idea from each chapter on a notecard. Once you are done reading look back over them as a reflection piece.

Post reading: The questions for discussion that were designed by the author, Mary Amato, are a great way to engage in conversation after reading. Some of the questions include:

- Trevor's mom is always saying, "Rise above it." Describe several specific challenges that Trevor faces and how he uses his own resources to "rise above" each challenge.
- What do you think Trevor wants in the beginning of the book? What do you think he wants at the end of the book? Explain how and why you think he changed.

Extensions: The author has designed extension activities, curriculum connections, and interdisciplinary lessons. They all can be found on Mary Amato's website.

G6–8 Lesson Plan #2

Focus: Foster care, family dynamics, economics.

Book Title: *The Great Gilly Hopkins* by Katherine Paterson.

Before reading: Discuss types of families and experiences of children living in foster care. Look at the cover and read the description. What are some predictions that students can make about Gilly Hopkins?

During reading: While reading, take notes on each charter to develop a character profile. What are their likes, dislikes, actions, and maybe even predict their thoughts.

Post reading: Recreate the story ending. Discuss why the author chose the ending and decide how you might change it. Why would you change it that way?

Extensions: There is a movie that came out with the same name. As an extension, watching the movie and doing a compare/contrast to the book would be a way to bring in interdisciplinary concepts and higher order thinking. Additionally, a resource that can be used is a discussion guide that can be found at the Harper Collins (publisher) website.

G6–8 Lesson Plan #3

Focus: Family, friendship, resilience, hunger, poverty, homelessness.

Book Title: *Crenshaw* by Katherine Applegate.

Before reading: Discuss homelessness and poverty. Reflect on being hungry and not having a place to call home. Additionally, discuss each student's support system. Who do they rely on when something is hard or tough?

During reading: Throughout the reading reflection on the use of Crenshaw (an imaginary cat). Why does the main character rely on Crenshaw? What do you think Crenshaw provides? Furthermore, there may be some unfamiliar words in the book so take note of those and look them up throughout the reading.

Post reading: Jackson and Robin had to have one small bag of things to keep. Reflect on how that might make them feel. What would you take or put in your keepsake bag? Also, reflect on the name "Crenshaw." Why did Jackson give his imaginary cat that name? Finally, talk about the family relationships. Who is taking the most responsibly? Who seems to have the power? Why?

Extensions: A resource that can be used is a discussion guide that can be found at the MacMillan (publisher) website.

G6–8 Lesson Plan #4

Focus: Homelessness, empathy, parent death.

Book Title: *Paper Things* by Jennifer Richard Jacobson.

Before reading: Discuss the concept of couch surfing and the various forms of homelessness. This will provide a foundation for students to understand some of the situations in the book. Additionally, discussing the concept of empathy and what empathetic characteristics are will also provide some background knowledge for students.

During reading: Journal write your thoughts, feelings, and reactions to the occurrences in each chapter. Each chapter brings to light something interesting and being able to realistically and authentically reflect on the situations will add to the overall understanding of the book, and the development of personal empathy.

Post reading: There are discussion questions that are provided on the Candlewick Publisher website, however having students visually share the process of reflecting and journal writing throughout the story would add to the depth of reflection and knowledge. Some discussion questions are as follows:

- Gage leaves his home and takes Ari with him. What personality traits lead him to make this decision? Do you think he is a good brother?
- Daniel creates a bucket list. What thinks would you like to do before you leave your current school?

Extensions: A resource that can be used is a discussion guide that can be found at the Candlewick Press website.

GRADES 9–12

Teacher reflection: High school students are able to read, comprehend, ask high level questions, lead discussions, and reflect on books as compared to one's own life. Therefore, while using these books help students relate to their own life and widen their view of the real world. If you have students who have or are experiencing similar events as the characters, use this as a place of growth, reflection, and understanding that poverty and homelessness exist everywhere. It may not be fair or equitable, but there are coping strategies that can be learned and implored.

G9–12 Lesson Plan #1

Focus: Economics, low wage jobs, working poor.

Book Title: *Nickel and Dimed: On (Not) Getting By in America* by Barbara Ehrenreich.

Before reading: Discuss the various forms of poverty, focusing on the working poor. Engage students in the reflection process of how people may feel in those situations. Feelings may include anxiety, dread, and fear. How might current political situations impact the working poor in America?

During reading: While reading the book have students develop questions to research further. While this book was written many years ago, there are still current topics. However, ensuring that students know how to research the concepts of the book for current policies is important.

Post reading: After reading, engage in small group discussions focused on the book. Some discussion questions may include:

- Ehrenreich found that she could not survive on $7.00 per hour—not if she wanted to live indoors. Consider how her experiment would have played out in your community: limiting yourself to $7.00 per hour earnings, create a hypothetical monthly budget for your part of the country.
- Many campus and advocacy groups are currently involved in struggles for a "living wage." How do you think a living wage should be calculated? And, how do you think students can advocate for the working poor?

Extensions: Have students design a budget and provide them with various types of salaries. Can they survive for a month? Also, have them engage in playspent.org. After each activity have the students reflect on the experience and how this informs them at a local and national level.

G9–12 Lesson Plan #2

Focus: Resilience, homelessness, poverty, drug-addiction, AIDS.

Book Title: *Breaking Night: A Memoir of Forgiveness, Survival, and My Journey from Homeless to Harvard* by Liz Murray

Before reading: Research what the slang term "Breaking Night" means. Discuss/predict why the book has that in the title. What does it mean to forgive? What does I mean to survive? Do you think anyone can move from homelessness to Harvard?

A factual discussion of AIDS also needs to take place since that is brought up in the book.

During reading: Make a chart with three columns. Throughout each chapter keep a list of what you believe to be her successes (column 1) and failures (column 2), and then in the last column write how she used her success or failure as a learning block in her personal and educational career.

Post reading: Once the class is finished reading the book encourage students to come up with their own questions and discussion points. High school students are at the point to facilitate their own learning and questioning. Allow that process to happen in the classroom.

Extensions: Predict what the author is doing today. Then, research where the author is now. There are many videos and articles about where she is now. Have students see if their predictions were accurate. Why did she choose the path that she is on?

G9–12 Lesson Plan #3

Focus: Homelessness, poverty, tragedy, optimism.

Book Title: *Sorta Like a Rock Star* by Matthew Quick.

Before reading: Talk about the role of humor and optimism in life. Why do students in your class use humor? Do they enjoy humor? Why or why not?

During reading: Develop a brainstorming web of the people who come in and out of Amber's life. Why does she gravitate toward some people and why do some people exit her life? How do you think this impacts her?

Post reading: Discuss questions that are provided on several discussion guides, some of which include:

- How is Amber able to keep her homelessness a secret? What does the secret say about Amber? Her community?
- Why does Amber choose to speak the way she does? How would you react to Amber if she was a peer in your classroom?
- Where does humor come into Amber's life? Why do you believe she includes humor in her life?

Extension: Complete a character analysis for each character in the book.

G9–12 Lesson Plan #4

Focus: Self-esteem, homelessness, hunger.

Book Title: *Tyrell* by Coe Booth.

Before reading: Reading the information about the book on the back cover or online (summary), what are some decision you think Tyrell is going to have to make throughout the book? Do you have to make similar decision in your life?

During reading: If you were Tyrell, what would you write in your journal after each chapter? Put yourself in his shoes and try to think about what are his deep dark secrets and thoughts that he would share in a journal? It can be in poem form, music form, drawing form, or any type of form that you believe Tyrell would use.

Post reading: Tyrell has a love of music. Bring in concepts of Hip Hop Pedagogy as a way to extend and engage in the reading. There are several items available on the internet if you search "Hip Hop Pedagogy," one that can begin the process of incorporating it into your classroom is *Sparking Engagement with Hip-Hop* on the edutopia website by Joquetta Johnson from May 1, 2017.

Extensions: Think about the author's perspective. Do you think the author wrote this book for kids like Tyrell or for kids who are different than Tyrell? Why?

References

Aces too high. (n.d.). *ACEs science 101*. Retrieved from https://acestoohigh.com/aces-101/

Ali, R. (2019, September). *Football players give classmate new clothes after he was bullied for always wearing the same outfit*. USA Today. Retrieved from https://www.usatoday.com/story/life/parenting/2019/09/16/kid-bullied-wearing-same-clothes-gets-new-items-classmates/2340069001/

Ambrose, S. A., Bridges, M. W., DiPietro, M., & Lovett, M. C. (2010). *How learning works: Seven research-based principles for smart teaching*. Jossey Bass.

Amer, R. (2018, September). USA Today. *Hear the story of Chicago residents fighting against mountain of debris dumped near homes*. Retrieved from https://www.usatoday.com/story/news/investigations/2018/09/24/city-new-podcast-usa-today/1403927002/

American Institutes for Research. (2020). *National center on family homelessness*. Retrieved from https://www.air.org/center/national-center-family-homelessness

American Psychological Association. (2020). *Education and socioeconomics status*. Retrieved from https://www.apa.org/pi/ses/resources/publications/factsheet-education.pdf

American Psychology Association. (2020). *Effects of poverty, hunger and homelessness on children and youth*. Retrieved from https://www.apa.org/pi/families/poverty

Anderson, T. (2014). *Road tested: Three ways to engage parents in high-poverty settings*. ASCD Education Updated. Retrieved from http://www.ascd.org/publications/newsletters/education_update/sept14/vol56/num09/Three_Ways_to_Engage_Parents_in_High-Poverty_Settings.aspx

Åslund, C. (2009). Social status and shaming experiences related to adolescent. Overt aggression at school. *Aggressive Behavior, 35*(1), 1–13. doi:10.1002/ab.20286.

Boghani, P. (2017, November). *How poverty can follow children into adulthood.* PBS Frontline. Retrieved from https://www.pbs.org/wgbh/frontline/article/how-poverty-can-follow-children-into-adulthood/

Brandpoint. (2018, October). *Fighting the good fight: 5 misconceptions of U.S. Poverty.* The Associated Press. *Retrieved from* https://www.apnews.com/8986c60 fd1a440aa92e51400f3f4ebde

Carter, S. B. (2013, November). *The tell tale signs of burnout... Do you have them?* Psychology Today. Retrieved from https://www.psychologytoday.com/us/blog/high-octane-women/201311/the-tell-tale-signs-burnout-do-you-have-them

Center for Poverty Research (University of California, Davis). (n.d.). *Who are the working poor in America?: Data from the Bureau of Labor Statistics.* Retrieved from https://poverty.ucdavis.edu/faq/who-are-working-poor-america

Center for Poverty Research (University of California, Davis). (n.d.). *What is the current poverty rate in the United States?* Retrieved from https://poverty.ucdavis.edu /faq/what-current-poverty-rate-united-states

Chapin Hall at the University of Chicago. (2017). *Missed opportunities: Youth homelessness in America: National estimates.* Voices of Youth Count. Retrieved from https://voicesofyouthcount.org/wp-content/uploads/2017/11/ChapinHall_V oYC_NationalReport_Final.pdf

Collins, C. (2015, October). *For kids, living in poverty is living with chronic trauma, experts say.* Kera News. Retrieved from https://www.keranews.org/post/kids-livin g-poverty-living-chronic-trauma-experts-say

Compassion International. (2020). *Poverty defined.* Retrieved from https://www.com passion.com/poverty/what-is-poverty.htm

Cunningham, N. J. (2007). Level of bonding to school and perception of the school environment by bullies, victims, and bully victims. *The Journal of Early Adolescence, 26*(4), 457–478. doi:10.1177/0272431607302940.

Derman-Sparks, L. (2020). Addressing inequity with anti-bias education: Learning about economic class and fairness. *Teaching Young Children, 13*(3), 20–24.

Derman-Sparks, L., LeeKeenan, D., & Nimmo, J. (2015). *Leading anti-biased early childhood programs.* Teachers College Press.

Economic Policy Institute. (n.d.). *Poverty.* The State of Working America. Retrieved from http://www.stateofworkingamerica.org/fact-sheets/poverty/

Educational Research: Newsletter & Webinars. (2018). *Fighting poverty with empathy.* Retrieved from https://www.ernweb.com/blog/fighting-poverty-empathy/

Erdoğdu, M. Y. (2016). Parental Attitude and Teacher Behaviours in Predicting School Bullying. *Journal of Education and Training Studies, 4*(6). doi:10.11114/jets.v4i6.1459.

Family and Youth Services Bureau. (2012). *Practical application of the McKinney-Vento Act.* Retrieved from https://www.acf.hhs.gov/sites/default/files/fysb/mckven app20120829.pdf

Fink, L. (2016). *Culturally relevant pedagogy.* National Council of Teachers of English. Retrieved from https://www2.ncte.org/blog/2016/02/culturally-relevant-pedagogy/

Finkelhor, D., Ormrod, R. K., Turner, H. A., & Hamby, S. L. (2005). Measuring poly-victimization using the Juvenile Victimization Questionnaire. *Child Abuse Neglect, 29*(11), 1297–1312.

Firestreel. (2014, September). *Homelessness and academic achievement: The impact of childhood stress on school performance.* [Blog]. Retrieved from http://firestee lwa.org/2014/09/homelessness-and-academic-achievement-the-impact-of-childho od-stress-on-school-performance/

Firesteel. (2014, September). *Homelessness and poverty in public education system: An intro to our blog series.* [Blog]. Retrieved from http://firesteelwa.org/2014/09/ homelessness-and-poverty-in-the-public-education-system-an-intro-to-our-blog-se ries/

Firesteel. (2014, September). *Hungry, scared, tired and sick: How homelessness hurts children.* [Blog]. Retrieved from http://firesteelwa.org/2014/09/hungry-sc ared-tired-and-sick-how-homelessness-hurts-children/

First Things First. (2020). *Why early childhood matters: Brain development.* Retrieved from https://www.firstthingsfirst.org/early-childhood-matters/brain-de velopment/

Fisher, G. M. (1997). *History of poverty thresholds.* U.S. Department of Health & Human Services. Retrieved from https://aspe.hhs.gov/history-poverty-thresholds

Gaines, L. V. (2018). *Schools are using poverty simulations to build empathy. But do they work?* WillRadio.TV.Online. Retrieved from https://will.illinois.edu/news/stor y/schools-are-using-poverty-simulations-to-build-empathy-toward-the-poor.-but

Gay, G. (2013). Teaching to and through cultural diversity. *Curriculum Inquiry, 43*(1), 48–70.

Gleason, K. A., Jensen-Campbell, L. A., & Ickes, W. (2009). The role of empathic accuracy in Adolescents' peer relations and adjustment. *Personality and Social Psychology Bulletin, 35*(8), 997–1011.

Glor, J. (2019, March). *How a laundry room revolutionized a New Jersey high school.* CBS Evening News with Norah O'Donnel. Retrieved from https://www.cbsnews. com/news/how-a-laundry-room-revolutionized-newark-new-jersey-west-side-high -school-2019-03/

Gorski, P. (2016). Poverty and the ideological imperative: A call to unhook from deficit and grit ideology and to strive for structural ideology in teacher education. *Journal of Education for Teacher, 42*(94), 378–386.

References

Gorski, P. C. (2018). *Reaching and Teaching Students in Poverty: Strategies for Erasing the Opportunity Gap.* Teachers College Press.

Green, P., & Haines, A. L. (2011). *Asset building & community development.* Sage Publications, Inc. [Third Edition].

Gundersen, C., & James P. Z. (2014). Childhood Food Insecurity in the U.S.: Trends, Causes, and Policy Options. *The Future of Children,* 24(3), 1–19.doi:10.1353/foc .2014.0007.

Habitat for Humanity. (2020). *What is poverty?* Retrieved from https://www.habitat. org/stories/what-is-poverty

Heidary, F., Rahimi, A., & Gharebaghi, R. (2013). Poverty as a risk factor in human cancers. *Iranian Journal of Public Health,* 42(3), 341–343.

Henderson, T. (2019). *Poverty grew in one-third of counties despite strong national economy.* PEW Research. Retrieved from https://www.pewtrusts.org/en/research -and-analysis/blogs/stateline/2019/12/19/poverty-grew-in-one-third-of-counties- despite-strong-national-economy

Henig, R. M. (2018, June). The age of grandparents is made of many tragedies. *The Atlantic.* Retrieved from https://www.theatlantic.com/family/archive/2018/06/this -is-the-age-of-grandparents/561527/

Henion, A., & Holt, T. (2014). *Cyberbullying affects rich and poor alike.* Michigan State University Today. Retrieved from https://msutoday.msu.edu/news/2014/ cyberbullying-affects-rich-and-poor-alike/

Hiemstra, R., & Brockett, R. G. (2012). Reframing the meaning of self-directed learn- ing: An updated model. *Proceedings of the 54th Annual Adult Education Research Conference,* Saratoga Spring, 45, 155–161.

Homeless Connections. (2020). *What is homelessness?* Retrieved from http://hom elessconnections.net/homelessness/

Huang, J., & Barnidge, B. (2016). Low-income children's participation in the National School Lunch Program and household food insufficiency. *Social Science & Medicine,* 150, 8–14. doi:10.1016/j.socscimed.2015.12.020.

Human Rights Campaign (HRC). (2020). *New report on youth homeless affirms that LGBTQ youth disproportionately experience homelessness.* Retrieved from https:// www.hrc.org/blog/new-report-on-youth-homeless-affirms-that-lgbtq-youth-dispro portionately-ex

Jaggi, S. (2019, January). *The many forms of homelessness.* [Blog]. Retrieved from https://joinpdx.org/the-many-forms-of-homelessness/

Jensen, E. (2009). *Teaching with poverty in mind.* ASCD.

Jensen, E. (May, 2013). *How poverty affects classroom engagement. How student progress monitoring improves instruction—Educational leadership.* Retrieved from www.ascd.org/publications/educational-leadership/may13/vol70/num08/ How-Poverty-Affects-Classroom-Engagement.aspx.

Jolliffe, D., & Farrington, D. P. (2006). Examining the relationship between low empathy and bullying. *Aggressive Behavior: Official Journal of the International Society for Research on Aggression, 32*(6), 540–550.

Kaiser, T., Li, J., Pollmann-Schult, & Song, A. Y. (2017). Poverty and child behavioral problems: The mediating role of parenting and parental well-being. *International Journal of Environmental Research and Public Health, 14*(9), 981.

Khan, S. (2010). Prevalence of food insecurity and utilization of food assistance program: An exploratory survey of a Vermont middle school. *Journal of School Health, 81*(1), 15–20. doi:10.1111/j.1746-1561.2010.00552.x.

Kids in Need. (2020). *School ready supplies: Providing backpacks of supplies to students.* Retrieved from https://www.kinf.org/programs/srs/

Klampe, M. (2019, February). *Nearly two-thirds of American children live in asset poverty.* [Blog]. Synergies: Oregon State University. Retrieved from http://synergies.oregonstate.edu/2019/nearly-two-thirds-of-american-children-live-in-asset-poverty/

Kumar, G. (2018). *What is poverty and its types?* Retrieved from https://www.jagranjosh.com/general-knowledge/what-is-poverty-and-its-types-1523453034-1

Lareau, A. (2014). *Unequal Childhoods: Class, Race, and Family Life.* University of California Press.

Law Hawaii. (2018). *The law of homelessness: Definition.* Retrieved from https://law-hawaii.libguides.com/c.php?g=421172&p=2875672

Lester, L. (2012). Adolescent bully-victims: Social health and the transition to secondary school. *Cambridge Journal of Education, 42*(2), 213–233. doi:10.1080/0305764x.2012.676630.

Liu, L. (2012). Environmental poverty, a decomposed environmental Kuznets curve, and alternatives: Sustainability lessons from China. *Ecological Economics, 73*(15), 86–92.

Making Caring Common. (2018). *For educators: How to build empathy and strengthen your school community.* Retrieved from https://mcc.gse.harvard.edu/resources-for-educators/how-build-empathy-strengthen-school-community

McKernan, S.-M., & Ratcliffe, C. (2002). *Transition events in the dynamics of poverty.* The Urban Institute. Retrieved from https://aspe.hhs.gov/report/transition-events-dynamics-poverty/permanent-income-and-life-cycle-hypotheses

McKee, A. J. (2020). *Broken windows theory.* Britannica. Retrieved from https://www.britannica.com/topic/broken-windows-theory

McLeod, S. (2018). *Maslow's hierarchy of needs.* Simply Psychology. Retrieved from https://www.simplypsychology.org/maslow.html

McSweeney, K. (2019, March). *This is your brain on Instagram: Effects of social media on the brain.* Now. Retrieved from https://now.northropgrumman.com/this-is-your-brain-on-instagram-effects-of-social-media-on-the-brain

Middleton, J. (2015). *Addressing secondary trauma and compassion fatigue in work with older veterans: An ethical imperative.* Journal of Aging Life Care Association. Retrieved from https://www.aginglifecarejournal.org/addressing-secondary-tr auma-and-compassion-fatigue-in-work-with-older-veterans-an-ethical-imperative/

Mindtools. (2020). *The ladder of inference: How to avoid jumping to conclusions.* Retrieved from https://www.mindtools.com/pages/article/newTMC_91.htm

Missouri Community Action Network. (n.d.). *The poverty simulation.* Retrieved from http://www.povertysimulation.net/about/

Moore, C. (2020, February). *Resilience theory: What research articles in psychology teach us?* [Blog]. PositivePsychology.com. Retrieved from https://positivepsyc hology.com/resilience-theory/

Murphy, H. R., Tubritt, J., & Norman, J.O. (2018). The role of empathy in preparing teachers to tackle bullying. *Journal of New Approaches in Educational Research, 7*(1), 17–23. doi:10.7821/naer.2018.1.261.

National Center for Education Statistics. (2019). *Concentration of public school students eligible for free or reduced-price lunch.* Retrieved from https://nces.ed.gov/ programs/coe/indicator_clb.asp

Nickerson, A. B., Mele, D., & Princiotta, D. (2008). Attachment and empathy as predictors of roles as defenders or outsiders in bullying interactions. *Journal of school psychology, 46*(6), 687–703.

Noddings, N. (2005). *Caring in education.* Infed. Retrieved from http://www.uvm. edu/~rgriffin/NoddingsCaring.pdf

Parrett, W., & Budge, K. (2015, December). *How do we talk about poverty in schools?* Edutopia: Education Equity. Retrieved from https://www.edutopia.org/ blog/educators-need-understand-about-poverty-william-parrett-kathleen-budge

Poag, G. (2018, November). *What is the difference between acute trauma and chronic trauma?* [Blog]. Brentwood Wellness Counseling. Retrieved from https://www.bre ntwoodwellnesscounseling.com/single-post/2017/07/26/What-Is-The-Difference-Between-Acute-Trauma-And-Chronic-Trauma

Poverties. (2011). *Effects of poverty on society, health, children, and violence.* Retrieved from https://www.poverties.org/blog/effects-of-poverty

Rankin, J. G. (2016, November). *The teacher burnout epidemic, Part 1 of 2.* Psychology Today. Retrieved from https://www.psychologytoday.com/us/blog/much-more-common-core/201611/the-teacher-burnout-epidemic-part-1-2

Rozalski, M., Stewart, A., & Miller, J. (2010). Bibliotherapy: Helping children cope with life's challenges. *Kappa Delta Pi Record, 47*(1), 33–37.

School of Social Welfare: The University of Kansas. (n.d.). *The strengths perspective in social work practice.* Retrieved from http://socwel.ku.edu/strengths-perspective

Smeeding, T., & Thevenot, C. (2016). Addressing child poverty: How does the United State compare with other nations? *Academic Pediatrics, 16*(3), 67–75.

Sparks, S. D. (2016, August). *Student mobility: How it affects learning.* Education Week. Retrieved from https://www.edweek.org/ew/issues/student-mobility/index.html

Stevens, B. (2018, June). *Buddy benches foster sense of inclusion among kids on local school playgrounds.* Herald Courier. Retrieved from https://www.heraldcourier.com/lifestyles/buddy-benches-foster-sense-of-inclusion-among-kids-on-local/article_f765f8e8-6b70-11e8-8419-db997a1428cd.html

Stopbullying.gov. (2017). Ohio anti-bullying laws & policies. Retrieved from https://www.stopbullying.gov/resources/laws/ohio

Stroud, G. L. (2017, November). *Achievement gaps are just the symptom. Opportunity gaps are the real problem.* [Blog]. Education Post. Retrieved from https://educationpost.org/achievement-gaps-are-just-the-symptom-opportunity-gaps-are-the-real-problem/

Study.com. (2020). *Anti-bullying: Definition & policy.* Retrieved from https://study.com/academy/lesson/anti-bullying-definition-policy.html

Sweeney, E. (2018, August). *The problem with school lunch: How the wealth gap is shaming our students.* The Huffington Post, TheHuffingtonPost.com. Retrieved from www.huffingtonpost.com/entry/school-lunches-wealth-gap_us_5b72ee42e4b0bdd0620d0b43.

Tapp, F. (n.d.). *Teacher burnout: Causes, symptoms, and prevention.* [Blog]. Hey Teach! Retrieved from https://www.wgu.edu/heyteach/article/teacher-burnout-causes-symptoms-and-prevention1711.html

Teaching for Change. (2020). *Anti-bias education.* Retrieved from https://www.teachingforchange.org/anti-bias-education

The Jason Foundation. (2020). *Youth Suicide Statistics.* Retrieved from http://prp.jasonfoundation.com/facts/youth-suicide-statistics/

The Kids in Need Foundation. (2020). Retrieved from https://www.kinf.org/programs/srs/

The Salvation Army. (2020). *Homelessness fact sheet.* Retrieved from https://www.salvationarmy.org.au/about-us/our-services/accommodation-and-homelessness-services/homelessness-fact-sheet/

Toldson, R. A. (2019, January). *Why it's wrong to label students 'at-risk'.* The Conversation. Retrieved from http://theconversation.com/why-its-wrong-to-label-students-at-risk-109621

Toolshero. (n.d.) *Ladder of inference.* Retrieved from https://www.toolshero.com/decision-making/ladder-of-inference/

United Steelworkers Political Action Fund. (2017). *New study finds startling rate of poverty among working-class families.* [Blog]. Retrieved from https://m.usw.org/blog/2017/new-study-finds-startling-rate-of-poverty-among-working-class-families

University of Minnesota. (2016). *How does nature impact our wellbeing?* Retrieved from https://www.takingcharge.csh.umn.edu/how-does-nature-impact-our-wellbeing

Vedantam, S., Benderev, C., Boyle, T., Klahr, R., Penman, M., & Schmidt Jennifer. (2016, November). *How a theory of crime and policing was born, and went terribly wrong.* [Podcast]. NPR Hidden Brain. Retrieved from https://www.npr.org/2016/11/01/500104506/broken-windows-policing-and-the-origins-of-stop-and-frisk-and-how-it-went-wrong

Voss, J. M., & Lenihan, S. (2015). *Fostering resilience for children living in poverty: Effective practices & resources for EHDI professionals.* [Issues Brief]. Retrieved from http://www.infanthearing.org/issue_briefs/Fostering_resilience_in_children_living_in_poverty.pdf

Waters, S., & Mashburn, N. (2017). An investigation of middle school teachers' perceptions on bullying. *Journal of Social Studies Education Research, 8*(1), 1–34. Retrieved from https://login.libproxy.siue.edu/login?url=http://search.ebscohost.com/login.aspx?direct=true&db=eric&AN=EJ1141984&site=ehost-live&scope=site

Watson, A. (2019). *The 2x10 strategy: A miraculous solution for behavior issues?* [Blog]. Retrieved from https://thecornerstoneforteachers.com/the-2x10-strategy-a-miraculous-solution-for-behavior-issues/

Wilson-Simmons, R., Jiang, Y., & Aratani Y. (2017). *Strong at the broken places: The resiliency of low-income parents.* [Policy Report]. National Center for Children in Poverty. Retrieved from http://www.nccp.org/publications/pdf/text_1177.pdf

Wlodkowski, R. J., & Ginsberg, M. B. (1995). A framework for culturally responsive classroom. *Strengthening Students Engagement, 5*(1), 17–21.

Wong, H. K. (n.d.). Teach expectations and student achievement. Retrieved from https://www.effectiveteaching.com/userfiles/cms/unit5Files/42/GoBe49TeacherExpectationsandStudentAchievement.pdf

About the Authors

Anni K. Reinking is a former professor and current education consultant located in Illinois. She specializes in early childhood education and multicultural education. She currently provides training in topics focused on poverty, trauma, multicultural education, and developmentally appropriate practice. Her research agenda has consistently focused on multicultural education and social justice. She has published or presented research in the areas of multicultural education, challenging behaviors, trauma informed practices, creating positive school cultures, and more. She is a member of multiple state and national organizations focused on multicultural education and early childhood education.

Theresa M. Bouley is professor of education at Eastern Connecticut State University. She specializes in reading/language arts and teaches courses primarily in early literacy and reading and writing development, pedagogy, and assessment. Her research agenda has consistently been focused on multicultural education and social justice. She has published or presented research in the areas of multicultural/multiethnic literature and literacy, environmental care and social justice, LGBTQ+ issues such as the inclusion of same-sex families in children's literature and gender identity and expression in young children, empathy education and bullying, and more. She is a long-standing member of the National Association for Multicultural Education (NAME) and is president of NAME's state chapter in Connecticut.